Praise for
Practically Divine

"These are the moving stories of broken women and wounded communities healed by the immense power of practical love. No one knows more about redemption than author, pastor, activist, and speaker Becca Stevens. Having herself experienced the trauma of sexual abuse, poverty, and death, Becca has spent decades working for and with women survivors. It's a life spent in unconditional service and joyful faith. *Practically Divine* is a prayer book, a manual for living with an open heart."

—Isabel Allende,
activist and bestselling author

"I have a prediction, or rather three predictions. If you read this book, you will: (1) See the power of love in a whole new light. (The real thing, not the Huey Lewis and the News song, though they are both excellent.) (2) You will think, "I bet I would be great friends with Becca Stevens!" (3) You will visit Thistle Farms and volunteer as fast as you can. How do I know? Because that's what happened to me and dozens of other people I've taken on field trips to this special part of Nashville. Book your flight before you crack this book open, because once you start reading, it's going to be hard to ignore the practically divine."

—Jon Acuff,
New York Times bestselling author of *Soundtracks: The Surprising Solution to Overthinking*

"This extraordinary book just might be Becca Stevens's best … and that is saying a lot! Like the healing oils from her famous Thistle Farms, *Practically Divine* is gentle, powerful and, yes, very practical indeed. Open these pages and prepare to experience the practice of love, a balm for your soul."

—The Most Rev. Michael B. Curry,
Presiding Bishop of The Episcopal Church and author of
Love Is the Way: Holding on to Hope in Troubling Times

"Becca's experience in building community while creating a justice enterprise make her the perfect guide to lead us down a path toward discovering our own impact. With *Practically Divine*, she writes exquisitely about the stories of women who have overcome and risen up while weaving in her own mother's sayings with both wisdom and humor. Along the way, she brings her reader into a grounded awareness of the wisdom we each carry within us."

—Jessica Honegger,
founder of Noonday Collection and
author of *Imperfect Courage*

PRACTICALLY
DIVINE

PRACTICALLY DIVINE

BECCA STEVENS

HARPER HORIZON

Published by Harper Horizon, an imprint of HarperCollins Focus LLC.

Any internet addresses, phone numbers, or company or product information printed in this book are offered as a resource and are not intended in any way to be or to imply an endorsement by Harper Horizon, nor does Harper Horizon vouch for the existence, content, or services of these sites, phone numbers, companies, or products beyond the life of this book.

Scripture taken from the Holy Bible, New International Version®, NIV®. Copyright © 1973, 1978, 1984, 2011 by Biblica, Inc.™ Used by permission of Zondervan, www.zondervan.com. All rights reserved worldwide. The "NIV" and "New International Version" are trademarks registered in the United States Patent and Trademark Office by Biblica, Inc.™

This is a work of nonfiction. The events and experiences detailed herein are all true and have been faithfully rendered as remembered by the author, to the best of her ability. Some names have been changed to protect the privacy of the individuals involved.

ISBN 978-0-7852-4175-1 (eBook)
ISBN 978-0-7852-4174-4 (HC)

Library of Congress Control Number: 2021930940

Printed in the United States of America
21 22 23 24 25 LSC 10 9 8 7 6 5 4 3 2 1

I dedicate this book to my siblings, who came through our childhood with humor, compassion, and the ability to "snap out of it" long enough to do the real healing work.

Katie Ruth (RIP),
Sandra Lynn,
Pamela Jean,
and Gladstone Hudson

I love that we carry on Mom's work in our stories, our work, and through our children.

To the poet, to the philosopher, to the saint, all things are friendly and sacred, all events profitable, all days holy, all men divine.

—RALPH WALDO EMERSON,
Essays, First Series

Contents

Introduction

STANDING IN A GERANIUM field, smelling the
dark soil fertilized by rabbit poop, is different from reading about the healing properties of geraniums. Walking
beside a woman in a refugee camp holding a rag over her
baby's face because so much dust rises from the dry, red
dirt is different from imagining how hard it is for moms in
camps. Experience is nine-tenths of love. The senses of
the beholder transform information into compassionate
experiences that are holy.

Too much ink is spent on trying to perfect an ideal of
love, which is wholly impractical since love is revealed
through experience. We learn about love's many facets,

including humility, mercy, forgiveness, joy, and grief, through experience. The experiences of the practically divine shared in this book come from love stories I have picked up, like sacred bread crumbs, in which divine love can be seen, tasted, and smelled right in the midst of extraordinarily ordinary—and sometimes extraordinarily horrific—days.

Stories and experiences ground the idea of the practically divine and offer a way for us to glimpse how we all are practically divine and in the presence of great love. Those experiences can sometimes be scary and lonely, but they also leave us knee-bucklingly grateful. In the stories scattered throughout the book, I am sharing the moments I was able to recognize the divine love that was present through it all. Such a recognition can be wildly freeing and creative.

•　•　•

MY MOTHER WAS a great inspiration to me. When I was five, my father was killed by a drunk driver, and my mother was left to care for five young children. Despite being poor and alone, she served as a powerful example of how to find the divine love surrounding us, by tending to practical needs through arts and crafts and in her wise sayings:

"Come to find out . . ."

"Three moves . . ."

"God is love—don't worry about the rest."

Her sayings didn't feel like platitudes but practical bits of knowledge that could keep us going. Some were antiquated, so they kind of lost their punch, like "This whole thing is a shambles," since most of us don't know what a *shambles* is (think *mess* or *wreckage*). "You will grow up to be a ne'er-do-well," meant to be a threatening statement to all the kids draped over furniture watching TV, to get us off our butts and help. Her sayings rise in me like fragrance from a lavender sachet tucked away in a drawer. As the drawer is cracked open, all of a sudden you are awash in a scent that stirs your heart. I can still hear her voice, fresh and present like those old lavender buds, thirty years after her death.

My mother's example of showing love through practical means gave me the wherewithal to open a home for women survivors of trafficking, prostitution, and addiction more than twenty-five years ago in Nashville, Tennessee. It was a small house for five women. I said: "Come live free for two years with no authority living with you. Live free." I did it because I figured that's what I would want if I were coming in off the streets or out of prison, where people were telling me what to do all day. I didn't do it because of my mom or because of the childhood sexual abuse I experienced at the hands of a church elder, though all of that was a part of it. I did it because sanctuary is the most practical ideal of all.

I wasn't interested in repackaging charity in shiny, new boxes with the latest words. I was bored by trendy cause-hawking that left me feeling disconnected. I was disillusioned by a bifurcated political system that numbs compassion. I wanted to do the work of healing from the inside out. And that begins with a safe home.

Imagine, for a moment, a small seed of hope lying dormant in your heart. You hold on to it, despite trauma and injustices you may have faced since you could spell your own name. One day, you arrive safely at your new home and allow community to be like the soil, and resources to act like sun and water, so, finally that tiny seed grows into a stunning plant, scattering blossoms of love hundredfold.

From its humble beginning, Thistle Farms now has thirty global partners that employ more than 1,600 women. In the United States alone, Thistle Farms has more than fifty sister communities offering free, two-year housing. The global artisan survivors are creating revolutionary crafts that help restore their communities. The mission to be a global movement for women's freedom is broad and is growing exponentially, come hell, high water, or pandemics.

Initially, it seemed a bit ridiculous to me to think that by starting a small community, we could somehow change the world, but now, it seems more ridiculous to me to think that somehow the world will change if we *don't* do something.

Now, I can see that one loving gesture is practically divine. We have to do small things and believe a big difference is coming. It's like the miraculous drops of water that seep through mountain limestone. They gather themselves into springs that flow into creeks that merge into rivers that find their way to oceans. Our work is to envision the drops as oceans. We do our small parts and know a powerful ocean of love and compassion is downstream. Each small gesture can lead to liberation. The bravest thing we can do in this world is not cling to old ideas or fear of judgment, but step out and just do something for love's sake.

●　　●　　●

I AM WRITING this book for everyone hungry to taste the divine, struggling to see it, needing inspiration and challenge to go back out and try again. You can cross lines and gain new perspective. It is possible to love the whole world. We don't have to get cynical, fearful, numb, or be shamed into thinking we have nothing to offer. I think sometimes it's even much easier than we think.

I have sat through way too many presentations in which a speaker will say something like, "Here are the Four *C*s to a fulfilling life." We take out our notebooks or laptops to write down or type the four *C* words. We can't help ourselves. Then the next night, I lie in bed and think of three of the words, tossing and turning, trying to recall the fourth. By the end of the week, I'm lucky if I remember that the words started with *C*.

There is no secret formula to experiencing the sacred ∫ in our lives. *It just takes practice and practicality.* The deep truth of our lives and the fullness we are striving for don't happen with someone giving us the code to deep knowledge. Meaning and faith are not secret things. Sometimes what we need most is to remind one another of how the divine is all around us, calling us to see and taste it for ourselves. We can find our deep truth and purpose while we are on the way to the grocery store or struggling to make a marriage work. We can find beauty while we go through a TSA checkpoint or walk along any sidewalk. We can feel gratitude sitting in a waiting room or forgiving ourselves for one thing we didn't get done.

Practice might not lead to perfection, but it will lead us closer to love. When we cultivate our ability to see the divine in the midst of our days, slowly we can trust that deep within us lies the same love that was woven into creation.

I have felt the practically divine all along the way of my personal journey. Even when I didn't know where I was headed, or I worried that a new justice enterprise would be too much to take on, I knew I had to do something. It is good news that, beyond our power to fully understand, our path is full of sacred crumbs that are enough to keep us moving in the right direction.

It doesn't matter where we are—whether we are reading this in the comfort of our bed, on a prison cot, or wandering in the world—something divine is present at any given moment. Maybe it's just an idea, a moment of inspiration, or even the song of a bird. We can learn from one another's collective wisdom, but we also have to be willing to forge our own way to new places. All we have learned, felt, and thought from childhood until this moment is with us as we take the next step. We have all we need to make that next step, with no regrets. *We do not need more thought leaders repackaging ideas into a marketable gimmick or bumper-sticker theology. We need to help one another with real, hands-on advice to root us and help us grow.* The practice of love in our thoughts, words, and deeds would serve businesses, politicians, and pastors well. *Practically divine* is what it sounds like: both practical and divine. We are both *almost* and *usefully* divine!

People are searching for the divine. Think about the divine and where you can find it in your life:

Through accepting your present state,

Finding beauty in the brokenness,

Embracing the divine chaos of the unknown before you,

Redefining the old lies and stories you've been told, so you can learn from the past and move forward,

Using your creativity to reconnect to your divinity and to others,

Finding love's presence even on your most difficult days,

Appreciating the divine gifts that come from your imperfections and traumas,

Letting go of your physical and figurative baggage,

And finally sharing in a feast of love, knowing there is always enough mercy and forgiveness to go around.

Practically divine is not an oxymoron. It is as poetic as being optimistic in the midst of depression or as vital as sitting in silence with a friend who can't take any more advice. It is both and, not either-or.

Most people want to feel excited about their ability to do something that will create meaningful change. This inspiration comes with one simple, small, practical act of love. When I see how love has healed so many broken people, including me, it is my great joy to remind people how they can create love in the world.

When you spread the message that love heals and that signs of divinity are all around, supporting us on our darkest days, you pick up lots of friends. It's a message that gives people the impetus to do something, anything, so we can share in the feast of love together. Now is the time to promote the practically divine idea that in coming together, wherever we are, we can lift one another up and be happier and more creative.

You just have to keep practicing. The results are always a surprise, with more unfolding than you imagined, teaching you that you can't go back the way you came. Practically divine asks us to find a new way.

In this book, I will write the word *love* over and over. Please know that it's shorthand for my whole theology. When I say *love,* you can translate that into "life with God." To me, love is where the temporal and the eternal meet, and love has an infinite number of expressions. Love is done a disservice when it is categorized into neat boxes, and the million shades of its blessings are missed. The love I'm exploring in this writing is love that feels practical and specific. I am pursuing the kind of love that moves from ideals into practices that take on flesh and bone.

PRACTICALLY
DIVINE

| ONE |

In Broad Daylight

"CAN YOU BELIEVE IT?" my mom would ask with indignation to whoever was in earshot. "Right there, in broad daylight." Somehow, in her mind, the fact that she was cut off in traffic or was shortchanged was worse because the infraction happened right there *in broad daylight*. The phrase emphasized that the perpetrators were worse because they had no shame and did whatever they were doing, right there, in the light, instead of skulking around in the darkness of shadows and moonlight. I can see the palms of her hands lifted toward the heavens, with a slight shrug of her shoulders that always came at the end of her pronouncements.

Many adult children can recall with amazing accuracy the ghost of their mother's voice. We conjure up our mother's old sayings seemingly out of the blue, with the same internal timbre, decades after they were first uttered as we received lessons we never asked for. One minute you're an adult, and in a flash of thought, quick as lightning, your instinct kicks in and your mother's old sayings strike through time, crash through hours of therapy, and zap you with words ringing inside your head. Just thinking about my mom this very second brings waves of sayings into my consciousness. It makes me wonder sometimes if she's sitting on a cloud just above my head, throwing sayings like lightning bolts to keep me on track.

"You need to set goals for each day," I can hear her saying when I was a teenager, above the hum of her vacuum cleaner at 6:00 a.m. on Saturday mornings. She ran the machine around my bed like an alarm. "Do you think laundry does itself?" might be the next sentence coming from her overworked and financially strapped lips. On Saturdays, she would have mowed the grass and started the bread baking before she woke us up, vacuuming as she got ready for the grocery store. I kid you not. She didn't tire. She found the divine in the practical, and her theology was summed up in simple, pragmatic phrases that stick with me like sitcom theme song lyrics. "We are dirt and angels," she'd muse as she tried to find the divine in the practical daily chores of keeping a family afloat on less than a living wage. There were no retreats or vacations. Just sweet, practical ways of finding wonder and joy.

* * *

"DON'T MAKE ME come in there!" I can hear her yelling from a distant room in the back of my mind.

Why would I make you come in here? I remember thinking. That would be ridiculous since you are in a bad mood, and I haven't done whatever it is that I was supposed to.

"You'd better snap out of it," I can hear her retort emphatically when one of the five kids (Katie, Sandy, Pam, Gladstone, and yours truly) she was raising alone was "falling apart" or "having a meltdown."

"You made your bed," meaning no matter the situation, don't complain, because you got yourself into it. Now it's time to deal with it.

"Who promised you fair?" was her answer to any one of her kids when someone whined that something wasn't fair relative to the siblings.

"People can't make you feel anything. How you feel is your choice," she'd say if something happened at school.

"We go through heaven and hell right here—no need to wait" was one of the things she'd say when things were getting desperate on the financial front. "If you don't like it, you can pack your bag, and I'll help."

Dear Lord, Mom. So much advice for a kid.

Things fell apart in our family on quite a few fronts after a drunk driver killed our dad and left us poor and vulnerable. A lot ensued as the traumas were layered like cake tiers held together by filmy sheer will and a bunch of tried-and-true sayings. She did keep us together, and now

I think those sayings were as much for her as they were for us.

She was a practical, thirty-five-year-old widow who threw her beloved sayings out to us like an inheritance. I can be sitting in a meeting or preaching a sermon or talking with my own children, and those sayings pop into my head. It's all I can do to not say them out loud. "If wishes were horses," I remember her saying when I was too needy, "beggars would ride." So much for childhood dreams.

I wonder if she was being prophetic when she sighed long ago, "If it's not one thing, it's another." Maybe she had a vision thirty years into the future and was prophesizing about the endless podcasts people are recording. Recording podcasts used to be a special occasion. It was like taking a break from work and sitting down to talk with a friend. But now, it *is* the work. Social media influencers, churches, old-school radio personalities, and thought leaders need to communicate with their audiences by podcast. Podcasts are the media fashion of the season. I get it—I am a part of that world. I want to be supportive of podcasts. In fact, I believe there are great things about the democratization of media. Everyone gets to put their messages out there, then people choose to whom they listen. But podcasts are time-consuming, both to produce and consume. And truly, all you can say is, "If it's not one thing, it's another," accepting that we will always be busy doing something. Before podcasts, it was going door-to-door, and before that it was scribes, and before that it was trying to figure out how to make fire. If it's not one thing, it really is another.

*   *   *

I RECORD MOST of my podcasts from the café at Thistle Farms in Nashville, Tennessee. The café is an important part of the community I founded, because it's the place where the community is invited to help share the good-news story of how love heals. The café is a big part of my own story, so I love doing the podcasts there. The added benefit is that all the podcasts help draw business to the café. So, that is where I was sitting as I was waiting for the people interviewing me to finish setting up.

I was already hair-and-makeup ready, which for me means I washed my hair and put on mascara. Anytime I do that, I hear the comment, "You look so good today—what did you do?"

"Shower," I answer.

I have the feeling that the older you get, the more you gotta step up and try a bit harder. As we age, it's not just our skin that gets coarser. It's our hair, it's our voice, it's our optimism. You have to do a little more work to keep your hair silky and your creeping skepticism in check. I know the team that works with me secretly conspires to buy me clothes that arrive at my door as "presents."

I can imagine the members of my advisory board saying maybe they could help a sister and their cause out a bit by making her come across less coarse. They think I could do a better job of spreading the word of how communities heal if I could maybe come across a bit softer in both my appearance and my tone. It's hard, though, because my natural state is hoodie, leggings, UGGs (if I have to wear shoes), homemade socks, and quick conversations. It is not that I don't want to look more put together or pleasant—it's that I'm too lazy to pull it all together. And the other problem is that I love that part of myself. I think homemade and cozy things are beautiful, and banter and freewheeling wit are gifts. But I do see their point. I see that I am representing them and others, and I need to not lead with my thorny thistle parts but with the softer center that can wear florals.

While I was sitting at the café with my hair looking silky and wearing a black turtleneck, my assistant walked up and said, "There's someone at the counter who wants to talk to you."

"I'll talk to them later, Kristin."

"He said he's your mother's godchild."

I began scrolling through the contacts stored in my memory, but no godson of my mother's popped up. "I don't know him, Kristin, and if he is an old godson of my mother's, it's not good news."

My mom's godchildren would have come from our old church, St. Matthias, the mission church my dad started before he was killed. We stayed on at that small, dysfunctional church until it was finally razed to build a grocery store when I was about eighteen. I never really understood why Mom stayed at the church after my dad died, except that because she was so new to town and so young, with five kids, maybe those were the only people she knew. Maybe she stayed because it was one of the threads she could hold on to that connected to my dad. She was widowed at thirty-five with five kids and, to the best of my knowledge, never even went out on another date.

When I say the church was dysfunctional, I do not use that term lightly. That church was where my abuse began. From the elders to the youth workers, it was an unhealthy place that thrived on secrecy. I remember my mom going to court once, to testify on behalf of one of the women in the church who'd shot her husband. We had an event called "slave day," where the youth were auctioned, and we had to spend a day doing whatever the person who'd "bought" us told us to do. Those are just two examples of how messed up this church was. This also was a church that would flip out if the liturgy wasn't perfect or the choir robes weren't pressed.

When the church was demolished to make space for a grocery store at about the exact time I left for college, they held a service to "deconsecrate" it. Even then, though I hadn't put together the whole idea of what *dysfunctional* meant, I knew enough to think, *This is a waste of time.* It was desecrated when I was six and first molested in the fellowship hall. I was relieved when I saw the huge yellow bulldozer take the whole thing down. *Finally*, I thought, *it will be a place that feeds people and offers something useful.*

"Go talk to him," Kristin insisted. "He's standing right there."

I couldn't make out the guy from where I was sitting because his back was to us as he faced the counter. He was standing below a huge sculpture comprising hundreds of teacups hanging from the ceiling.

The teacups dangle on varying lengths of threads, creating an eight-by-six-foot wave of cups. The cups represent survivors from around the world. We started off building a small chandelier with about fifty cups. Those cups were collected along with individual stories. We'd take a photo of the story and the cup and then hang the cup. Tea was central to my thoughts of what it means to live practically divine. It is healing, it is ritualistic, and it is very pragmatic. It has value, sates thirst, and builds community. I wrote a whole book about the way of tea and, along with oils, have made those the cornerstones for what it means to live practically and spiritually grounded.

As mentioned, those first few cups contained the stories of remarkable women survivors. One was from a ninety-five-year-old Japanese woman who had been in an incarceration camp in World War II. Her cup, which is still on display, is stamped with a Japanese logo for a company whose products were banned from being imported to the United States during the war. There is one cup that a woman sent in, which told the story of her heroic grandmother who survived the brutality of an older relative and ran away to make a home for her mom. She donated one of her grandmother's old chipped cups, reminding us of the beauty in brokenness. One of the treasured cups came from the child of a survivor in Bosnia who was able to flee the genocide. The story came with the beautiful message that surviving, too, takes its toll.

The teacups represent the café's founding principle, that we need to show hospitality to all. Every cup has a story, and every person walking through that door is carrying a story. Our job is simply to welcome them and offer them a sweet cup of healing tea.

I couldn't very well not say hi to my mother's godson while he stood beneath the cups, a place to welcome all, to share stories and feel accepted. Not welcoming him would fly in the face of everything I had built, even if I knew his presence somehow meant trouble. Just the idea of him made me remember that hard period of childhood. My siblings and I are very close, and we have a group text that's our virtual connection. I knew no matter who this visitor was or what bridge I was getting ready to recross, I could text them and they'd help me remember correctly and get some perspective.

"This won't be good," I said to Kristin as I got up and told the podcaster I'd be right back.

The visitor turned toward me, and I almost recognized him through what felt like some kind of wrinkle in time carrying me back more than forty years. He looked familiar, in a bad way. He looked like and was the same age as the man who'd abused me.

He introduced himself and said, "I'm your mother's godchild."

I asked him who his grandfather was, and when he said his name, I stopped breathing for a couple seconds.

While I knew there was no way he could know his grand-father had been my first abuser, it did throw me for a loop, as my mother would say. A couple seconds is plenty long enough for me to compose rapid-fire questions. Why did he come find me? Does he know? Why was he standing *right there, in broad daylight*? I could hear my mom say those exact words as she played the narrator to this story for a second.

While the events of our past do not change, our per-spectives on them do. What might have scared the living hell out of me at six years old, standing with a thirty-five-year-old man now felt like some kind of karmic mo-ment I needed to pay attention to. There he was, the de-scendant of my molester, at the same age my molester had been, standing before me, a woman twenty years his se-nior. You can do this challenging math. What was once a feeling of being lost and scared was now being trans-formed into something else. What I couldn't figure out, standing before him, was what that something else was. But I didn't want to miss this practically divine moment, in broad daylight, by jumping to conclusions.

He was the spitting image of the man I remembered so much about. I could look at him and see his grandfather, the first time he took me alone and made me sit in his lap. I could almost feel his breath on my neck as he held me tight, one hand on my flat six-year-old chest and the other pulling down my underwear. I didn't have any words to describe at the time what was happening to me, but I had them now. And just like I could conjure up my mother's voice, I could conjure up the horror of the acts of his grandfather, with mountains of words.

In my next exhale, I could remember how his grandfather's hands were always moving in gross rhythms. I could see his thick, greasy hair. The olive complexion that still somehow looked pasty, with thick glasses reflecting sweaty skin.

As a million thoughts bolted through millions of nerves, signaling me to either run or freeze, I mustered the composure to ask calmly, in my pastor's voice, "Why are you here?"

I was betting he didn't know his grandfather had been my abuser, and that meant he didn't know the trauma his ancestor had inflicted was a big reason we were standing in this café. It didn't feel ironic; it felt like poetic justice. He didn't know that because of his grandfather a half a century earlier, I'd had a hard time functioning as a priest when I'd started my work. He likely didn't know that, for many abused kids, the experience opens the door for creepy older guys to enter their lives, such as through school and internships. There was no way this young man could know the shame and the burden of secrecy I carried that made me more comfortable hanging with the women I was supposed to be helping on the streets than with my pastor colleagues. There was no chance this stranger could imagine the hard grounds of sexual abuse his grandfather had made me travel, that his grandfather had blurred all the lines for me between priest and prostitute (if there ever was a line), and it lead me to search the streets to meet my sisters and find a way for us to heal.

Why is he coming in here? I thought about a thousand times between the sentences he was speaking, about his story and struggles. He couldn't have known I was feeling like my six-year-old self, because he shared his grandfather's smile.

Twenty years earlier, if I'd met the son instead of his grandson, it would have triggered an overwhelming response in me. But I gave up the word *trigger* years ago—it feels too violent and scary and outside my control. Instead, I like to think of things that pop up in broad daylight as *uncoverings*.

The grandson uncovered something in me, and now I had to decide how to respond. All his presence did was awaken something I knew already. *Broad daylight* can mean that we're able to see something more clearly, that it's a safe space to revisit old, haunted grounds. Broad daylight may be the biggest gift as we search for what is divine in our day.

In some ways it's a gift to see what lurks just below the conscious self. I could choose, in that moment, to bury all the memories and tell the guy to get lost. I could choose to confront him and let the whole thing ruin the day. Or I could choose to look the memory straight in its ghostly eye and see it for what it was. I could face this in broad daylight, with the assurance of a huge community of survivors standing with me. I was seeing him under a wave of testimonies, in the form of cups, reminding me of love's shape. I was talking to him at the counter, where within ten feet there were baristas, servers, and cooks, all survivors who have lived through more than I can imagine. This was just a meeting, and I didn't need to make "a mountain out of a molehill," as my mom would have said I tend to do.

You can go ahead and fill in the million questions that raced through my head. Did he do to you what he did to me, when he was an older man? Did you do to anyone what he did to me? Why are you coming to me? Do you have any idea what your family cost my family?

All these questions dwelt in a space I was holding between breaths, and I couldn't let them spring forth from my lips, which were choosing words as carefully as the right peach in a pile. I wasn't bringing any of those questions up. For God's sake, we were just standing at the café counter, where in a couple minutes an interviewer was going to ask me about my abuse and why I'd started Thistle Farms.

"I am here, because I want to volunteer or something. I want to help." He said his family had talked about the work of Thistle Farms, and while he'd been in rehab, something in him made him want to come and see it. He had followed a hunch, and it had led him right here.

That was when the scene turned into a vision. His standing there in broad daylight, with the sun pouring down, was the opposite of chance. It was inevitable. All roads, before he was even born, led him to find his way to this counter, where he might get a cup of tea and begin to build a new foundation. His standing there didn't take away how his grandfather had broken me open and the pain that ensued for years, but I knew, like I know my children are my heart, that I could welcome him.

Right there, in broad daylight, we are given momentous moments that can lead us to love and freedom. It may take decades or generations, but we can find our way. With the echoes of my mother's voice like signposts, the hundreds of cups of tea in this place, the thousands of people who have offered me grace along the way, the small and big heartbreaks that kept me searching, and the beautiful weeds—all of that could bring me into broad daylight, to be visited by an old ghost reminding me how far I have come.

So, I stood face-to-face with him, with what I hoped was love. I had founded a community on the belief that Love Heals. If I believe that, then of course the children of the children also need to heal. If I want to believe that Love Heals, I can be generous in my forgiveness and work. I am no longer a child with no agency, living in the mercy of an abuser. I am older and safe and have enough love to give him.

Love in a world filled with practically divine moments kicks our ass sometimes, and at the same time feels like a miracle. I can almost imagine the well of gratitude that sprang from Mary as she sang her Magnificat: "My soul doth magnify the Lord." I could have sung my own magnificat:

For he has looked with favor upon all those who thought there was just acceptance and not healing. It may take generations, but love gets the last word. Love has shown the strength of doggedness that scatters the proud and powerful. Love lifts up the broken, opens them to compassion.

Love fills the hungry with crumbs gathered along the way, which have become a feast. Love is the remnant of all the mercy we have known.

But instead of reciting a magnificat, a phrase from my mom rushed into my head: *I can't believe I am meeting you here, right in broad daylight.* Fortunately, I didn't say that out loud. What I said was that I hoped we could talk again sometime.

I am my mother's child, to be sure. I can imagine that such an encounter, fifty years in the making, easily could have sidetracked me for the day, but there was too much to do. So, I think I reverted to my mom, who just pulled out a saying, took things in stride, filed them away, and kept going. I thanked him for stopping by and turned back to the podcast, probably taking a breath and remembering, "If it's not one thing, it's another."

I know I still have a long way to go to understand the practically divine, but it is a gift to pause for a moment to think about how far I have come. I love the idea that fate and chance have their place in this world, but also, some sweet signs point out the divine along the broken and messed up roads. It's the journey as well as a destination.

I don't think the injustices of this world and the trage-dies of life are part of a divine plan. That would make for a cruel God. But in spite of the injustices and horrors, where we are right this very moment, in broad daylight, is still a sacred place where we can experience a practically divine moment, in loving signs along our broken road. If we can learn to recognize and appreciate the divinity in these broad daylight moments, then we also can offer more love to other searching and hungry travelers. Broad daylight is the safest place to start a brave adventure, where we can leave old fears and stale beliefs along the roadside and venture into our own heart to discover how powerful and good we are. We all should be trying to get out into the broad daylight, and see the light and breathe the fresh air.

Deanna, a beautiful survivor leader, graduate of the Thistle Farms residential program, and fellow crocheter, recently told me the story of how she finally came in off the streets. Her story is sadly similar in theme and timeline to the horrible universal story of violence and abuse of children and the aftermath of that trauma. I think it's important, as you walk through this story with me, to keep in mind that, statistically, the women I walk alongside at Thistle Farms had been sexually assaulted by their tenth birthday. Deanna shared that story of childhood trauma, which is often a red carpet to early addiction, mental health struggles, and problems with the law and school. Without help, she could never have sustained a sober life, never have climbed what felt like a mountain of consequences from all the things done and undone.

A few years earlier, she'd come to live at Thistle Farms for about six months, but then ran back to the streets one night, when things felt too hard. She just couldn't handle it. After she left, one of the program's early graduates, Regina, who was the outreach director, went to the streets to look for her. When Deanna heard Regina's voice, she jumped into the bushes. She couldn't stand the idea of facing Regina in broad daylight. She said there was too much shame and fear. She felt she had to stay in the shadows of the bushes and use her last ten dollars to buy her last piece of crack and turn just one more trick. She could hear Regina's voice on the street: "Deanna, I know you are in there. You can come out when you are ready. We will still be here."

Over the next several weeks, Deanna said Regina's voice had ruined her high. She couldn't get the voice out of her head, and one of the women who had been with her on the streets left to go find Regina. A couple months later, Deanna emerged from the shadowy, scary, and violent bushes, in broad daylight, to find life.

Coming out into broad daylight to face our troubles and build something new is heroic. I applaud with great enthusiasm the hundreds of women who have graduated the two-year residential program and stood in the light. Deanna has taken years to build her new life, where she can stand and let the light shine on her. She resolved her court issues, got her small business making blankets up and running, and is mending her relationship with her kids.

Wherever we are today, it is good to stand in broad daylight and see exactly where we are, so we may glimpse where we might like to go. Standing in broad daylight helps us to live healthier and happier lives and take in the rich vitamins and clarity the light offers. There is a real thing that happens when we don't get enough light: it affects our ability to think and process. We need to be in broad daylight, good and practical and free.

Practically divine means taking stock of where we are right now, accepting our present state for all its beauty and brokenness, and then taking one practical action to help make the next phase better.

| TWO |

Lightning at the
End of the Tunnel

EMBRACING WHAT LIES AHEAD lands us in
a bit of divine chaos, but that is where new visions are
born. As we move forward, it helps every now and then to
glance into rearview mirrors, to remind ourselves we have
made it so far with grace. We can't know the outcome, but
we can trust the past that has led us right here and believe
that is enough to help us keep going. "Lightning at the end
of the tunnel" captures the apprehension we can feel
about what is coming down the pike.

I first heard this phrase from my sister, Sandy, a healer
and teacher who's had way more than her share of close

encounters with death. She has been life-flighted out of Cameroon, survived cancer, and worked two jobs her whole life. She is our mother's daughter, down to the snappy phrases she uses to explain everything. I loved that she never said *"light* at the end of the tunnel," but instead reminded us with humor that we're heading into the scary unknown where God knows what might happen.

She coined the phrase when she was finishing her doctorate in biophysics or some subject that sounds like biophysics. I am honestly too embarrassed to ask her again what her degree is in, because I don't want her to think I can't understand simple brain-science terminology. What she meant in the phrase was that, as dark and as bad as it is right now, don't lose your edge, because trouble may be up ahead. It's not meant to be a statement of doom and gloom—for our family, it stirs up feelings of excitement and wonder.

After all, this is my sister who, when the winds picked up and warnings of tornados were broadcast, told another sister, Pam, and me to go outside to fly a kite with her. It was the most magnificent kite flying I can recall. It required zero running to get the kite spinning like a whirling dervish. Up and up it went into the crazy, translucent, pre-tornado green sky, until the string ran out so fast Benjamin Franklin couldn't have held on to in his simple lightning storm, and my sister let the whole thing go as the kite sailed on to Kansas to land on ruby slippers. At least that was how wondrous it seemed. It felt like the threat of the lightning and the joy of the whirlwind were all tangled up together to weave a magical tale.

We still tell the story of flying the kite just minutes before a tornado touched down in south Nashville and lifted the shed out of our backyard and into our neighbor's crabapple tree. Something about the whirlwind and the unknown invites the divine to make appearances and create experiences that help us laugh, get through tough times, and plan for new adventures.

Often on new adventures, I see the lightning at the end of the tunnel. I have seen it in my work growing a global movement for women's freedom as I walk alongside women committed to healing their communities. I have seen the divine chaos strike like bolts of lightning, as a small group of women sit in a remote village and talk about global markets. I have felt it strike on a midnight flight to Rwanda, not knowing what day it was or how we were going to find the extra hundred thousand dollars to bring desperately needed irrigation to a geranium farming community, when out of nowhere an idea cut through fear and created a solution. These were all things I never could have imagined from the comfort of life on the safe side of the tunnel.

* * *

BEFORE THE GRANDSON left the café, the two of us said we might meet again after the beginning of the new year. I went back and forth between wanting to share the whole story with him and wanting to back out and walk away. After my first meeting with him, something wasn't right with me. No matter how I thought I'd shaken it off with ease, or that it was all good, it was sitting funny. One thing about survivors that I respect more than anything is that we don't "get over it." There is no getting over that abuse. It would be like asking someone who had an arm amputated to use both of their hands. We can adapt, and we can make our good arm really strong. We can do miraculous things, but we can't regrow a removed arm. I can't reclaim the innocence I lost at six years old. It's just gone. The way I understood the world and the way I saw older men changed forever. The scars will be with me even as I return to dust.

Every one of the women I serve shares the truth that we won't ever forget the past or get over the abuse. Things just don't go back to the way they were, so we won't get back what was there before the abuse. My mom was right—"No one can promise you fair." Over the years, I have come to celebrate the wonder of survivors, to revel in their strength, and to respect that the internal scars they carry remain.

When I traveled to Montgomery, Alabama, to see the Legacy Museum, I was moved to tears many times. It fired me up in my work, as I saw the injustices and lynchings faced by descendants of slavery in the past and present. As I stood there, I also felt weepy, because I knew the scars of many, many women can't be documented in the same way they were documenting these scars. While you can see whip marks on a back, you can't see all the internal, intangible scars of sexual assault. Those scars feel more like a burl that has wrapped itself around our most sensitive places, as a protective barrier. Burls form when a tree is injured. The burl wraps around the injury and attaches for life. It's intricate, with complicated knots, crazy swirls, and stunning twists. It's also the most valued piece of wood to use in creating bowls because of those elements. Once the burl forms, the wound beneath the burl heals and remains safely hidden. No one can see the original scar because the burl has protected it from further injury.

* * *

THE FOLLOWING SUNDAY morning, after I met the grandson in the café, another encounter sent me into a tunnel I couldn't avoid. I was preaching that morning, right before Christmas, about what it was like to meet my abuser's grandson in broad daylight in the middle of the café. About three-quarters of the way through the sermon, I saw, sitting in the third row to the left, among the 450 people in the congregation, the grandson. With an intense stare, he was listening to me preach about seeing him at the café, remembering his grandfather, and my coming to the realization that I could feel such forgiveness and love.

As I spoke, I wondered, *What the hell is he doing here?* Almost immediately, it dawned on me that his family probably never told him about his grandfather's history as an abuser, and this was a shocking way to hear about it. A queasiness rises from certain realizations, as they take hold of your body and squeeze. When you can't get away from something, it just makes you feel sick sometimes, as you wait for the lightning to strike. It's the same feeling I had the time I happened upon a grizzly on a trail in a national park. While our heart rate soars, we don't blink and we keep walking. We can experience those shocking realizations like lightning and not flinch. I had to finish preaching, and I felt his eyes on me for the rest of the service.

Afterward, he met me in the nave and was justifiably shocked and kinda mad. I told him I hadn't expected him to come to this church and obviously would have chosen to tell him before I preached about it. He told me that I'd both opened a can of worms and explained much. People in his family knew, I reminded him. I wasn't the only person his grandfather hurt.

Then, in what felt like a sharp left turn, he said when his grandfather died that he "got up and read the prayer of Pilot, as my grandfather wanted."

"When did he die?" I asked.

"More than fifteen years ago."

"Your grandfather was pretty scary," I said, to make sure he knew I wasn't apologizing for standing up for myself and being in solidarity with survivors, who are free to speak their truth. But I also had an overwhelming desire to offer him compassion, since he may well have gone through his own trauma, and I'd caught him off guard. He talked about some stuff that felt a bit scary. I won't share his story in this recounting, because while I defend my right to share my story, I don't share the stories of others without permission.

I wrote down my phone number and gave it to him, said he could text me when he was ready to talk.

"It's so strange to me that this is happening. I admired your mom and the good she did," he said. He then stated he had to call someone, and he left.

When I didn't hear from him for a few days, I felt myself traveling through a dark part of the tunnel in what feels like the opposite direction of practically divine. It was more like impractically paranoid. Hundreds of books have been written about this—it's where the heart of overthinking comes from—the place where professionals talk about old tapes playing in behavioral counseling. These days, folks in the know describe this as *living bravely* and *untamed*. All of that is firmly in the court of easier-said-than-done.

I was playing those old tapes full blast on speaker. A chorus of voices told me it was all going to hell in a handbasket. A band joined forces with the voices, as they sang, *no one ever really liked you much anyway. You are a bad person to traumatize the grandson.* To such music, many of our dreams shrivel and die in the desert of uncertainty and shame.

That place in the tunnel is big enough for just one. Tunnels can at first be wide enough to bring friends, then suddenly narrow into a cave you have to crawl through on your own. You can tell people what it looks like from inside, but you're the only one trying to get through it.

This kind of tunnel brings to mind a Thistle Farms graduate, a woman who was pregnant before her twelfth birthday and on the streets by the time she was fifteen. She is beautiful and amazing and still young, and she can enter tunnels so deep and dark you can't reach her. This last one she went down sent her to the hospital for surgery. In our last conversation, where there were laughter and tears as she described losing her wig in an alley, she said she couldn't quit beating herself up over her relapse. She said her shame and anger were killing her. She's still in the midst of that tunnel that has carried her back to the streets to do the same trade of the tricks. She may die in that old tunnel if she can't find her way out. All our hearts at Thistle Farms break for her collectively. We just can't get to her.

The tunnel I'm speaking of pales in comparison, but it's still my tunnel, and it's still plenty dark. All our tunnels are plenty dark. We don't really have to compare the darkness of one another's tunnels. For the next few days after my encounter with the grandson, my mind in the tunnel was wild in its imaginations. I conjured up various scenarios about what the grandson was thinking and what he was doing. I imagined that he hated me and was angry and somehow all I had done and built was going to come crashing down around me. I imagined he was writing a story about how I almost did him under, when he sat and listened to the sermon and heard, for the first time, what his grandfather was capable of.

It's remarkable to me that, for years, I've spoken and preached that we all have the freedom to tell our stories unapologetically, and that the sickness lies in the secrets. I forgot about the sickening feeling that comes in the aftermath of outing. I vividly remembered the day I went to my abuser's home, as I began the Thistle Farms community, and met with his wife and him. I started the whole meeting with, "I have a story to tell." After I told the whole story, which spanned several years, from the fellowship hall to the barn stall, his very first question—asked with some disgust and anguish from his pain—was, "Who have you told?"

Right after confronting the grandfather, I felt so proud of myself and compared it to lifting the heavy weight I'd carried deep in my body, handing it over to him, and saying, "You can carry it now—it's your turn." But in the days following the confrontation, I felt sick and hated that I felt like I had, as my mom would have said, "upset the apple cart." The same thing was happening all over now with the grandson, even though I knew I was doing the right thing and offering his family another chance for healing. It seemed impossible to me that the exact same feelings were all living inside me now, even though I wanted to believe I'm a somewhat wiser person.

After the brief encounter with the grandson at the back of the church, I went back and forth between righteous indignation and sorrow. I spun conversations around and around in my head until I was dizzy. I knew he should know what his grandfather had done. I knew he had his own story, and I needed to hear it. I also knew he was mad. I felt like I was resurrecting the anger and destruction of his grandfather and wondered how much of that the grandson had in him. I didn't know if I had further harmed him, which made me feel sick. And I didn't know if I could handle him at my chapel or at Thistle Farms in the fore-seeable future.

Right before the end of the year, we met again at the café. He told me some disturbing stories and confirmed some of the trauma in the church. However, he seemed angry and unconvinced that my abuse accusations were true and at one point even slammed his hand on the table. His anger scared me for less time than it takes for light-ning to flash, as I realized I didn't give a rat's ass if he was mad. If I'd survived his grandfather's physical abuse, this young man's anger wasn't going to put me back in my place of fear. So, I explained that it wasn't his choice, that he could ask his grandmother, because she knew the whole story—and it might be the thing he needed to find his own healing.

"Your grandfather was cruel and mean and violent," I told him. "You have to figure out the past, so you can live a different future."

"I need some time," he said, and we agreed to meet once more. I didn't want to sit down with him again, but I also wanted to make a smoother path and make amends for the way he heard the story, so he could find his way through in peace. I could imagine how dark and scary his tunnel was, and I hoped nothing but good for him.

●   ●   ●

THE NEW YEAR came, and I was grateful to leave for Ecuador for a couple of weeks. My hope was to infuse time and space into the tunnel, to shed a bit of light. That is where the great gift of trying to live in a more practical and divine way can save us. Sometimes there's no way to fix things, and no way to take stuff back. It doesn't all have to be fixed and wrapped up with a bow before we can do good works and get out of our own way. We can give ourselves enough grace to make some room for healing. Not fix it, just carve out room for healing to start doing its work.

Ecuador is the perfect place to carve out that room. For more than twenty years, Ecuador has been an epicenter of the practically divine for me. Through the work I get to do there, I can find the space to get out of my head and onto more practical matters. I can feel the rain without scrambling to get inside, see the stars while we sit around and play cards, and work on a scale that feels hopeful but not overwhelming.

This year, I was traveling to Ecuador to meet with a group of artisan survivors we had been working with for years. Twelve people—six Ecuadorians and six Americans—were on this four-day new year's retreat. Our goal was to help scale and structure with the sewing operation leaders.

These kinds of tasks don't always fill me with awe and gratitude, but they're a hell of a lot better than fretting over past injustices and current unsolvable relationships.

The hard part about developing partnerships with groups of artisan survivors overseas is that you know you're in for the next ten years. It's exciting to start a new justice enterprise, but along with it comes a sense of traveling together through a long tunnel. Working for justice isn't a quick fix. It's not a spring break "mission trip." To me, doing justice work alongside survivors feels more like growing a forest. It requires patient investing and long-term tending. We may never fully see the depth of the roots or the wonder of the canopy, but if we stay long enough, we may relax in the shade together. Sometimes the financial burden will rest on my shoulders, or something will happen requiring me to "pop" down to Ecuador to help. It's a gift to go to a place like Ecuador with a community and dive deep into work, but it's a gift that comes with a cost.

The justice enterprise was taking off for the six Ecuadorian seamstresses. They had successfully doubled their income in the past year, and their new eye pillows with essential oils had sold out twice in the past three months. It was time to have a full-on retreat at the Ecuadorian seaside facility and get this project to take off like a kite in a tornado.

During the four days of our trip, as we all committed to growing the line of hand-sewn products and finding new markets in Ecuador and the United States, we became "on fire," and I glimpsed the divine chaos that runs through the tunnel, as it whooshed us through. Like lightning bolts, ideas started flashing and were transformed into proto-types on the second morning of our retreat. Marketing plans were rolling off our tongues as we danced sponta-neously with joy. Every person was filled with energy that was less about ego and more about collective wonder. We came away with four prototypes, complete with models and branding strategies, like the new line of *bulsa*/tote bags on which the words, "I carry my sister's story" is em-broidered.

On the last morning, just as the sun rose over the Pa-cific Ocean, I took a long walk on the beach with another participant to reflect on what we had experienced. I felt so happy as I realized the significance of the trip. As I tried to pull my thoughts together, I understood that epiphanies are experiences that happen *to individuals*, but they al-most always happen *in groups*. That was an amazing dis-covery for me. It reminded me that even though the way through the tunnel can take us on narrow paths alone, it sometimes opens up, and we walk alongside others—and that's the place to see the wild lightning. One person might catch a brief sighting, then others start looking, and we see the amazing bolts as the whole tunnel fills with excite-ment and wonder. By seeking out community, we can expe-rience being swept up in something bigger than ourselves, even as we have our own personal *aha!* moment.

As I was describing my *aha!* moment to my friends Frannie and Tara, walking along the beach, we looked up a ways and saw a long line of fishermen. They were tethered together, hauling an enormous net, probably the size of a football field. Bound together in columns, several rows of men were tied together. But they weren't only tied together, walking backward to haul the net—they were moving sideways toward one another. They were bringing in their collective haul, far more than anyone could have caught alone.

As they formed an increasingly tight-knit community, hundreds of frigate birds starting descending and diving at the net. When you see a frigate bird up close, you can't help but duck. Its wingspan is almost eight feet. The frigate bird can't swim or walk, so it's an expert at low-flying twists, turns, and dives. They also nest in huge groups, and when they have a feeding frenzy along the shore, it feels a bit like a scene from Hitchcock's thriller *The Birds*.

If the scene in front of me was the vision of experiencing the practically divine in full color, the frigate birds played the role of the Spirit. The birds were swirling in the air, grabbing for anything, urging the fishermen to huddle in close and hurry up. We were laughing and dodging the birds as well. The bound fisherman had caught so many fish, there were plenty of smaller fish to offer the crazy frigates nosediving the nets and people, like lightning. It was magnificent as it reminded me of the rush of the Spirit coming in and asking us to work together in fast, practical ways, to reap what we could not on our own. In the face of the frigates, the fishermen acted in complete harmony, with speed and practicality. We need one another, and the stirring of the Spirit, to be our best practical and divinely inspired selves.

We emerge from our tunnels in a different place from where we started. In every story of faith, the Spirit comes as a surprise—it's more abundant than we imagined, and we can't go back to where we were. I came home from Ecuador in a different place. I knew with confidence I never had to go back down the same tunnel of fear and silence from childhood. I have been there, freaked out over that. I have clasped hands with my sisters, and I could invite the grandson, this broken and searching young man, to walk down his own tunnel with people who can help him. I was different after the trip. I don't know how, but it was almost as if I couldn't remember why I'd been so scared a few weeks before. I love the lightning flashing and the frigates diving and making it through to the other side and thinking: *I will never go back. I love it out here in the light.*

When I arrived home, I saw that he'd texted an old photo he'd found of my family in his family albums. I thanked him and gave him the number of a wise friend and counselor and knew fear wouldn't lead me to freedom— love in community would. I wanted to revel in the divine chaos of community, not feel stuck in some stupid tunnel. I could feel the wildness of the frigate birds in my spirit and wasn't going to let him or the other million tiny distractions quash the joy of coming out of the tunnel. I was done engaging him and knew that between the frigates and friends, I was once again out in broad daylight. I guess, in the back of my mind, I also knew it wouldn't be the end of the story, but it would be the end for the next while.

I went straight from Ecuador to the hills of North Carolina to speak at a gynecology convention, traveling in a rented minivan with two graduates of the residential program. Usually, when we're hired to speak at a convention, I offer a keynote, one of the women shares her story of healing, and the third woman sets up a product table, where we hope to sell thousands of dollars of products as people rush to the table after our session.

On the seven-hour car ride, I shared my recent experience of feeling like I had been in a tunnel and the wondrous reprieve I'd experienced in Ecuador. After we'd been talking for hours along the crisp, bare winter roads, I asked them what it feels like for them when old ghosts pop up or they feel themselves going into a tunnel. I wanted to know about the divine chaos they experienced.

One of the women, Leigh, told me an incredible story. Leigh has a kind face that rests in a smile. Her brown curly hair is always tossed into a messy bun that bobs in tenderness as she nods along with whatever you are saying. She leans into you, so you can feel better even as she shares her tragic story with remarkable honesty. In her brown eyes, you can also see a longing for family and friends who will stay with her.

Leigh was abused as a child and raped in high school. Then she was kidnapped by a pimp in Memphis, who shaved her head and held her prisoner. One day, she whispered in the ear of a john as he finished with her: "Please help me. I have to get out of here." After he left, he made an anonymous call to the police, who busted down the gate at the place where she and another woman were being held.

The police just put Leigh on a Greyhound bus with her shaved head and said, "Be careful." I don't think she could have seen anything but lightning in her future and could do nothing but duck away from the crazy birds above her. She told me story after story of how she struggled, lost herself and anything that meant anything, and knew she would die. She felt she'd never make it out of the tunnel.

But because of a friend of hers, she made her way to community at Thistle Farms. Knowing she had the time, space, and resources she needed made it possible for her to see that, with a community, she could walk through the long tunnel. We were her grounding, so the lightning wouldn't hurt her. From there, she could start to see her past with some perspective and walk into the broad daylight with a plan for her future.

Now when you ask Leigh how she feels about being practically divine, she laughs and, in her Southern twang, says, "Honey, I am all that and a little bit more today." Having the chance to work in a mission-driven business shifted something in her. When she tries to remember how the shift happened, she says she can't put her finger on it. Somehow she came through the other side of the tunnel. The biggest difference for her is that, for the first time, she understood what love felt like. She said she'd never felt love before, and feeling love now was her saving grace. She now has patience for other people and concern for the women still trying to do everything in their power to make it through one more day.

• • •

FATE AND CHANCE have their place, and sometimes lightning strikes, but divine mercy can be gleaned from the rubble of our brokenness after that lightning—whether we are carrying our grandparents' burdens, trying to heal from kidnapping and trafficking, or simply feeling a bit scared of what's ahead. I am coming to trust that the tunnel is not as long as we think. Beyond injustices and horrors, maybe we can still see a bit of flashing light at the end of the darkness. That is enough to remind us that there have been loving signs along our broken road. This understanding gives us the courage to be tender with ourselves so we can move forward.

We don't have to fear lightning at the end of the tunnel. In the practically divine, as we move forward, we can delight in the whirlwind and believe that in that space we may, every now and then and by God's grace, see visions. I think my mom was sometimes afraid of what might come. She had experienced so much loss. One night our house was broken into, and the thieves took some really crappy stuff out of our kitchen. My mom's comment was simply, "If they can live with it, I can live without it."

We can live into our future, knowing we will never ever have to live without love. And love can carry us through any storm. It would carry me through the next several months, reconciling my past and future in the present. It was going to be practically divine.

I n a world where practically divine thrives, there is space for ranting, waxing poetic, and uncoverings as we go about our days. Rants are not justified, fair, or reasonable. Rants are the topsoil we dig through to get to the richer soil that births poetry and movements. In living into the practically divine, there is great purpose in finding safe spaces to express rants, as long as we recognize them for what they are. They are not the truth, the last say, or our final feeling.

RANT #1: JUST BE NICE

I am angry about so many issues and systems, I feel like I have whiplash. It feels like each morning there is something to protest, boycott, fear, and rage about. But what I am the maddest about right this very minute is all the privilege and prejudice present in social service agencies. It has become a full-time job to be poor in this country. Especially during COVID-19, it is almost impossible for people to access what they need in the world of archaic systems that assume people are trying to cheat the system. The whole damn thing would be better if everyone who is making a living as a steward of other people's money, and whose only job is to distribute other people's money, imagined how they would want to be treated if they were getting out of prison or coming in off the streets and had to get a voucher, food stamps, or an ID. Stop being mean.

| THREE |

We Can Make It

SITTING IN A STEAMY tub with healing oils poured in can feel like a balm for weary souls. My bathtub is old, and I outfitted it years ago with a homemade shelf for typing on my laptop. While I am soaking in lavender-scented water, I am thinking about crafts. Buck naked in the dead of winter, I am visualizing a new owl pattern for knitted mittens that will save me time and still look amazing. That may seem mundane, in the midst of all the global injustices and personal hardships, not to mention the pile of work inside this laptop. Yet here I am, dreaming of mittens.

I'm not thinking about mittens apologetically. Instead, I consider them a vision of the practically divine. Seeing a new craft emerge feels as beautiful to me as a new melody arising for a musician, a new couplet for a poet, or a seamless equation unfolding for a mathematician. Arts and crafts can be how we experience the divine. Making things can be both an act of revolution and a means of healing. Think of Gandhi spinning cotton as a sign of civil disobedience. Think of the women whose children went missing during Chile's military dictatorship, who quilted their memories using swatches from their children's clothing. There are so many examples throughout time of people taking to crafts to make a new future. Dyeing cloth, pouring candles, and mixing oils are all biblical examples of the power of crafts to heal and change. People still find healing as they turn to crafting and creating. My friend with a leg broken in three places wrote to me last week about how she had started practicing her newfound love of watercolor painting while she convalesced. She said it has been one of the most healing elements of her six-month, non-weight-bearing life with two young sons, two dogs, and a full-time professorship.

Yesterday, I spoke on the phone with my colleague Abi Hewitt in London, who reported that forty-four women weavers are now in the refugee camp where together we started a justice enterprise called Love Welcomes, believing we could make something and thus make a difference. That number of weavers is up 60 percent from last year.

Love Welcomes came about after I saw a documentary on the horrific stories of women and children fleeing Syria. The scene I couldn't get out of my head was of an overcrowded boat with mothers clinging to their children and everyone crying. Most of the women's husbands already had fled and immigrated to Germany or Sweden. The boats the women boarded were too small and weak for the rough seas. People had to be rescued by volunteer sea captains from Greece and then taken to refugee camps, because other countries had closed their borders.

I tried to imagine what it might feel like to flee a war and board an unsafe boat on rough seas. There would be exhaustion, for sure, hunger as well. Frightened children who couldn't be comforted by their mothers, whose own hearts were pounding in their throats. Then they would land. The life vests would be discarded, they would be given a blanket, and the endless waiting would begin.

Watching and imagining their journey broke open my heart, which gets a little closed off sometimes. It was difficult to know what I could do to help. Too often we think the problem is too big for us to do anything. Or we think we're not up for the task. Then, one day, I was walking in the Tennessee woods, where so many ideas are born for me. As I thought about the women in the camps, an idea rose as quietly and quickly as a hawk on a thermal draft: *Let's weave the life vests they were wearing on those horrible boats into welcome mats.* The most practical and beautiful way to help seemed to be to take the symbols of the trauma and fear of their escape and turn them into mats that would be a new symbol of love and welcome for refugees. I had no idea how to use a loom or how to get the vests, but I loved the idea of welcoming refugees in a practical, deep way.

I started off by trying to figure out how to make a mat from a life vest. A friend acquired vests from a local canoe company, and I cut the fabric off the vests in strips and used a crochet hook to weave the strips together. It looked worse than some of my kids' summer camp crafts. But a couple months later, while I was speaking at a retreat center in North Carolina, I happened to meet a professional weaver weaving strips of cloth on a loom. We started talking, and I asked her to show me how to weave strips of life vests. When she agreed, I immediately went outside, found the head of maintenance, and asked if the retreat center had any life vests on the campus, since there was a small lake nearby. He said yes. I asked him if I could have one to tear into strips and, to my surprise, he gave me three.

After my next talk, I ended by holding up the horrible prototype I had crocheted and asked for a few volunteers to stay after and help me turn the three donated vests into strips, tie them together to make a long string, and see if we could weave them smoothly without fraying. The volunteers and I watched the weaver take the shuttle holding a whole ball of vest strips and weave them back and forth through the warp. The result looked like a stunning piece of theology and art woven together. To me, it was like looking at stained glass.

"Can you come to Greece?" I asked the weaver.

Without one moment of hesitation, she said yes.

Then Abi and I were off to California to secure funding, which happened over a single dinner with three friends, Wendy, Amy, and Frannie, who underwrote the entire enterprise. We were set.

In April 2017, Abi headed out a few days early and then picked up our group of seven from the Thistle Farms community in Athens, where we rented a car and drove out to a world unknown to us, of overcrowded and trauma-filled camps.

That first day in the refugee camp, I wasn't sure what to expect. Many big government agencies had told us that starting a weaving enterprise with Syrian war survivors was a bad idea. They cautioned us that hiring or paying refugees wasn't allowed because of their political status, and if we invited only nine women, there would be a riot.

The seven amazing women who accompanied us to the camp included a fellow CNN Hero from the previous year, who was a native Arabic speaker. She and Abi headed out into the camp to see if they could make some headway. The first woman they met had been in the camp six months and had started teaching herself English. She said she would help organize. Within the hour, we had nine women who volunteered to come, hear our proposal, and at least stay for the three-day training in weaving. It took another ten minutes to set up Venmo (a mobile payment service), so the women could be paid through their phones for their training time. There were both Kurdish and

Arabic women, all survivors of the horrific Syrian war, sitting side by side, considering the proposal to start a weaving enterprise together.

The camp was dusty and hot, a makeshift camp at an old military base. The few remaining structures of the military base were crumbling, with flecks of sea-green paint returning to the dust. As I sat there and tried to take it all in, I remember thinking: *No matter what happens, if we weave, we will be successful. No matter what barriers from outside and within this camp, no matter who leaves or stays, no matter if we ever make a dime, if we weave, there will be healing.*

Despite the pushback we had received, we fell into an amazing rhythm to the beat of the shuttle on the looms. By the end of our second day there, we had woven our first mat. But more important than completing the first mat was the fact that the nine weavers had already met and decided that part of their proceeds would be used to hire buses to help transport the more than one thousand people in the entire camp, to enable every person to get to Athens at least once every few weeks. Even before the first piece was completed, they were organizing and dreaming of how to help heal their community.

To create material for the mats, five women stripped the fabric from the bright-colored life vests. As they huddled in one corner of the United Nations High Commissioner for Refugees container where we'd set up our venture, one of the women said to her friends: "I hate looking at these vests. They make me so angry." The other women nodded in agreement.

This is a universal reaction I've observed in women's craft circles. One woman begins to express something, and everyone nods in agreement. When anyone describes what she is going through or how she feels, guttural sounds of understanding and acceptance rise from our collective throats. We listen and encourage as we sit together for hours with some mundane task. With this particular circle of women, the common experience was leaving their homes to cross the tumultuous sea in unsafe conditions. So, as soon as she mentioned the vest, all the women nodded and said, "Yes, yes."

One woman had been forced to buy three different life vests as she prepared to make her overseas journey, because the first two trips on the boat from Turkey to Greece were abandoned mere hours before the planned departure time. As she kept tearing at the material, she said she'd paid a hundred euros for the third one. What made her so mad was that she knew, and the smugglers knew, the life vests didn't even work, but the rule was that the smugglers wouldn't let you on the boat without a life vest.

She continued to shred the life vest as the conversation slowly turned away from the pain of the past and toward their children and what to cook for dinner. After hours of tearing those vests, every now and then laughter would filter through their stories.

Later on, I sat with a couple Kurdish women who rolled their own cigarettes. We reflected on the day of weaving, and they shared that their grandmothers had all been weavers. As we shared a strong, hand-rolled cigarette, they told me how, generations before, the Kurdish people had been known for their extraordinary weaving. But war and racism had displaced them, and they had forgotten they knew how. They expressed pride that they not only had done a great deal of work weaving the mats in the camp that day, but also had somehow connected across generations of their ancestors. I stood up, a bit dizzy from the strong tobacco, feeling so happy that I got to be a part of starting a justice enterprise in this camp.

•   •   •

BACK HOME IN Nashville, I soak in my tub and give myself the gift of imagining the communities of women in Mexico, Ecuador, Peru, Chile, India, and Haiti, all threading needles as they begin the day, ready to create new beautiful pieces as part of the global marketplace we've built together, which helps generate millions of dollars in income annually. The swirling images of crafts converted into housing and education, and the women sharing stories of trauma transforming into resilience, fill me with joy. I am happy that my passion has found a home and that I have lived long enough to begin to understand that arts and crafts are revolutionary tools for healing and justice.

Looking back, I now realize that arts and crafts are how my mom kept the peace. She would shoo us outside to collect pine cones so we could make scented fire starters. She made sure we knew our home was a lively studio, where we were free to melt crayons and make batiks without fear of dripping wax somewhere. We could collect eggs to paint, we could harvest plants for terrariums, and we could erect cardboard villages. Our world was safe and pretty, because she helped us learn that we could make it that way. Perhaps she knew that if she taught us how to make things, maybe we could make it through this world that had left us poor and traumatized. The crafts could bond us, give us confidence, and save us precious money.

Stories from all over the world, for all of history, reveal that arts and crafts are revolutionary. I remember holding an elaborate woven basket when I was a child. A missionary nun who worked in East Africa had brought it to my mother as a gift, while the missionary was in the States on leave. The weave of the basket was intricate. Instinctively, I must have known the tans and deep brown grasses reflected the land from which they grew. They were so much more lovely than the sad baskets we had woven ourselves, and I wanted more than anything to go and sit in that circle of women and learn how to weave that kind of poetic beauty. That basket was given an important place in our house as something exotic, something valuable, and something rooted in justice and mystery.

Creating is critical in healing and justice. Making crafts settles our bodies and minds, so we can listen and talk. Sharing stories over a beading project feels more like friendly chatter instead of a high-stakes, "tell your story" moment in a formal setting sure to evoke stress. When we can sit and know that we have five hundred more beads to string to make our creation, the stories feel comforting and help pass the time. When you have three hours to create something, fear subsides and memories surface. You don't even have to tell your story in chronological order. You can tell snippets of memories that surface and are released.

In the act of making things, we also find value in ourselves. We find ourselves admiring our own creativity and skills that maybe we had forgotten or never knew we had. We become proud of what we have made and delight in its beauty. If something we make feels beautiful, there is the possibility of beauty within the creator in us, the part of us that creates. There is even a bit of beauty we know we have now left in this world. If we have the skill to create and be healing agents, we don't have to wait for someone else to step in and do the healing work for us. We can be together and become the healing agents we have been longing for. While crafting doesn't replace the need for mental health professionals, it can be a great partner and remind us of our agency in the healing work.

Creating is hopeful and practical, and maybe even brings in some income. Because it is time-consuming and most of the work is mundane or repetitive, it can engage people of all ages and unite generations and families. Arts and crafts don't produce unattainable artwork that only a few individuals can achieve. In arts and crafts, we're just good hosts providing the needed tools and space to one another so creations can be made. Add to that formula hosting some capital and expanded markets, then arts and crafts flourish. In arts and crafts, we are creators who participate in the healing process. We don't have to be heroic problem solvers or control an uncontrollable environment. We get to create with old and new friends. The work of revolutionary crafting is respectful, it is historical, it is good. It is divine. It is that kind of work that balances the space between pragmatic and poetic.

I have been crafting and creating businesses for most of my life. One of the great inheritances I received from my mom was the gift of arts and crafts. I grew into believing I could create new things from the broken and discarded things in front of me—candles out of old Coke bottles and broken crayons, rugs from old T-shirts, and storage containers out of broken appliances, using simple, floral Con-Tact paper. Maybe I was born for the place where arts and crafts and justice intersect.

So it wasn't strange that I began the reality of the coronavirus pandemic in the middle of crafting in an asylum-seekers camp in Matamoros, Mexico. I had been on the road nonstop since Ecuador and was not slowing down anytime soon. I had trips to Australia, Hawaii, Toronto, Oaxaca, and Kigali booked during the next several months. I was in full-on mode when I got the news—it was time to quarantine.

About three thousand people are in a tent city on a dirt strip between the Rio Grande and the border with Brownsville, Texas. They have to stand in line to eat, to charge their phones, and to use one of the portable chemical toilets standing in a row that stretches the length of a basketball court. In what would be center court, there's a stand with a small table and a woman who is a kind of referee. As each person passes her station, she hands them five squares of pretorn and folded toilet paper.

At the time I was standing in front of the operation, I thought about the large-scale problems between governments and borders, and then the practical problems of people who just need some toilet paper and sometimes need more than five sheets. Of all the things and degradations I saw during the week I was there, that stuck with me, and I wondered if I could live on five sheets of toilet paper a day.

I was all geared up in the middle of March 2020, at the camp with a small group of women including my beloved friend Frannie, ready to launch a new venture with sweet dreams of revolutionary crafts, thinking I wouldn't worry about the pandemic and could keep traveling and working. I was going to launch a slogan for the women surviving in the camp: "We can make it." It felt perfect for starting a small crafting revolution on the border. I was inspired by the story of the artisan women from Oaxaca, who wear their hair in long braids with bright ribbons woven in. Their craft is pottery. Through their work, they have changed the whole community. Through spinning the clay from the earth, they have built schools, furnished houses, and changed laws. The violence and the gangs almost got the last word, but the women there speak: "We can make it." They inspire us to keep making it.

I sat under a shared tree, beading with about fifteen kids in the camp, listening to them laugh and tell stories with a resiliency we all should hope to embody in our lives.

A strong smell rose as the wind shifted, probably from some poor soul who couldn't wait in line to be called onto the court to receive the five sheets. This person, like hundreds before, must have gone down by the river and just squatted and wiped with thin, long grasses or stray leaves. I was smelling humility and longing—two things close to God's heart. I didn't cover my nose, but breathed it in like the kids did. I don't want to turn away from the smell of humanity or the reality of the struggle of families trying to find a home with their own damn bathroom.

Because of the pandemic, the Mexican government said the camp was shutting down to all outside visitors, effective immediately. We had about an hour to gather our stuff and walk across the border to the United States. The Mexican government was worried that since we'd flown down there, we could infect the camp. I felt sick that maybe I had put folks at risk, because I sometimes forget I can be stinky, infectious, and overstepping. The first lesson of the pandemic for me was humility. We can shift quickly from cries of justice with a global perspective to needing to shelter in place. As soon as we walked out of the camp, I started thinking about the days ahead and getting my own family safe.

My "We can make it" thoughts shifted to how I could help my family and friends back in Nashville make it. My sons would all be coming home. Within the hour, I was on the phone to buy a ticket home and then spent the next hour shopping online. Collectively, the whole world began thinking about how we can make it. Many of us started an internal list, planning for our gathering and distributing. We decided how we were going to spend our gift of time and not be the ones to gain the "corona twenty."

I had missed the toilet paper run and was shocked that people were hoarding toilet paper, so some folks didn't have any. People sure could have used a referee like the saint who stood between all the bathroom stalls and handed out sheets in the camp. I became that referee for my family, instituting toilet-paper-conservation pleas. I believe everybody would have fared much better in the toilet-paper shortages if we'd taken one roll at a time and used the camp standards, which would have allowed us all to feel toilet-paper rich. *So, when I say offering a roll of toilet paper to someone who is health compromised or economically poor is a spiritual discipline, I mean it.* It is holy and good. It is practically divine. It may be the sacrament of the coronavirus quarantine, the outward and visible sign of the inward and spiritual grace. The toilet paper example illustrated for me the difference in our spiritual lives between hoarding and sharing. The chasm that separates community and isolation. The first thing I wanted to do in response to the pandemic was start collecting and distributing toilet paper; a sign of the practically divine. In less than two weeks, I'd gone from sitting on *The Kelly Clarkson Show*, talking about our global movement and dreaming of new international partnerships, to collecting toilet paper for the women of Thistle Farms and their friends.

On my front porch, we started packing boxes with supplies, including homemade sanitizer and a roll of the sacred paper. Packing a box to give away a roll of toilet paper when you're down to your last eight rolls is a spiritual exercise. It is a tithe. *If you want world peace, maybe start by sharing a roll of toilet paper.*

The pandemic also has taught the world to exercise our creative muscles like never before. Crafters making masks have emerged as essential. Do-it-yourself folks are streaming on YouTube, ready to teach Johnny-come-lately how to cut hair, make homemade cleaners, create new recipes, and mix healing concoctions.

The first week of the lockdown, Nashville's mayor asked me to go on TV and speak to the community about why churches should no longer gather in large groups on Sundays. All I wanted to share with everyone is the simple message: "We can make it." We can make a new way and follow old traditions at the same time.

This is what I offered to the city of Nashville on those first few days of lockdown:

This is a new time for our community, but times of crisis are not new. There always have been times the prophets have said to weep, to laugh, to embrace, and to refrain from embracing. This is a time to refrain in love, knowing love can transcend six feet and that generosity can move with grace over distance.

Nashville is a community that shows up after storms and stays home to allow the work of our frontline heroes to carry the day. This is a time to be humbled by what we do not know and cannot see. It is a time to feel safe in the

hallowed green pastures of hope, not stuck in the shad-
owed valley of fear. We are a community that can worship
at private altars and among the tulip poplars, recognizing
the truth that whether in times to seek or in times to lose,
God is with us. We learn from every faith in every time and
purpose under heaven that the question in suffering is always: How long? The answer from our God, spoken by
Abraham, Moses, and Job, is "I am with you." While that
may not seem to be the answer we seek, it is the answer
that is sufficient. "I am with you as you ponder in the night
your big and small worries. I am with you as you share
your gifts in love with this community, even if you worry
there is not enough. I am with you through the times when
you weep and when you laugh. I am with you when you
mourn and when it is once again time to dance. I am with
you until the time comes on the other shore, where we embrace love forever."

The lessons of the coronavirus sabbatical continue to
humble and break my heart. But they are so rich. Through
my time I have learned the song of the hawk, although I
still haven't discerned her message. Every morning, I'm
grateful for safety and kind words. I have taken the time
to slow think and slow read and slow cook some of my
mom's recipes. I have also delved deeper into the ideas of
slow crafts and crafting from the remnants left around
my home.

We all have a natural inclination to create, but so much
of it is taken away from us as we exchange the creative

process for goods and services that are bought and sold. We think of arts and crafts as children's endeavors or decide we aren't good at it, so we forget how creative and practical duct tape can be or how much fun it is to paint on a wall. Because you fixed it or made it, it is more beautiful. I think about the candles sitting in my living room and, somehow, knowing how they were crafted makes them dance with holiness, and their light feels almost haloed. I love that things we make are better because of the stories that grow from the creative process, the joy that is made along with our creation, and the wonder that our two hands made something beautiful and useful. "We can make it" not only means we've got this, it means we're capable and can lean into our creativity, to feel the divine spark of wonder.

Here is the truth: I would rather make a rosary than pray one. But one is considered a spiritual practice and the other one arts and crafts. I want to blur those lines and all the lines that we have drawn between the sacred and what we have deemed the profane. Early on, I knew I had more in common with most of the women I have been in community with for the past twenty-five years than with most of the priests I have worked with. Arts and crafts and justice have blurred all the lines. The lines that separate priest from prostitute, you from me, are infinitesimally small, if they exist at all.

RANT #2: ENOUGH OF "EMPOWERING"

Recently, I was interviewing someone applying for a marketing position in the justice enterprise I work with in Nashville, Tennessee. This company, founded by women survivors in 1997, has scaled into a movement that helps employ a couple thousand women across the globe.

During the interview, the applicant said the reason he wanted to move from the Midwest to Nashville to work with us was to "empower the women" and "give them a voice." *Empower* is a trigger word for me. We all have those words and phrases that don't merely rub us the wrong way—they go against the grain of what we believe is just and good. Over the past decade, *empower* has become a word that sets off a rant inside me.

I stopped this probably kind and well-meaning young man and replied, with as much compassion as I could muster: "Do you think it's kind of ironic that you are using the word *empower*? I mean, when you think about it just for a minute, it is women survivors who started and grew this company, and we are interviewing *you* to come work for *us*. Since you're applying for the job, if we used your language, we are *empowering* you."

I stopped there, knowing I was starting a rant that has been developing for years inside my head and probably hurting his feelings. I don't like how easily I fall into rants. But, while I *am* ranting, let me say: the word *empower*, especially for women who have lived in systems that have tried to strip power since the first man put a crown on his own ego-swollen head, begins the conversation by reminding us that we don't have power.

To empower someone is to claim power independently for oneself. It is saying, without saying it directly: "I have more power than you. Because I am a moral person, I will give you a little bit of my power, but make no mistake—I will always have more power than you." Of course, that isn't what people necessarily mean or intend. However, it is the meaning implicit in the language, and I believe language is important.

Raised in trauma that included sexual abuse, poverty, and death, I never lost my voice or my power. It may have been muffled by fear, may have experienced static interference from the longing inside for forgiveness, or even been turned off by numbness or manipulation to get somewhere else. But I never forgot my own truth, and I never ceded my essential power.

When someone wants to empower another human, it seems that while his or her stance may feel open, the structures of power in place will not shift anytime soon. There is no sense of shared power or shifting in the systems that built power structures in the first place. I have seen it over and over. Women who have known the backside of anger, the underside of bridges, the inside of prison walls, the short side of justice, and the violent side of racism and sexism are applauded (and rightly so) for all they have endured, but silently, an empowerment looms in the clapping that fails to recognize the power in those women.

Women survivors in general have miraculously retained power and blended it with a resiliency this world needs. It's a gift when it's recognized as already there and not as something that someone has decided to give us. The remedy is threefold. To recognize the person in front of you as your sibling in life. To treat one another with mutual respect and do your work as you would want it done unto you. And to acknowledge the need for power shifts, not empowerment.

Okay, now I feel a bit better. It is good to rant it out sometimes.

Just don't say "empower," or I may start again.

FOUR

Come to Find Out

MY FAVORITE SAYINGS INCLUDE oxymoronic expressions, misquotes, and mash-ups. A blended saying, such as "up against a corner," brings me joy. A phrase like "We are not anticipating any emergencies" can stay with me for days. Just thinking about it makes me smile. Mash-ups like this one from my sister, "You can lead a dead horse to water, but you can't make him drink," brighten my day. My mom also used to say, "out of the frying pan, into the oven," which I thought meant it was time to take something off the stove and bake it. I didn't know the original saying until decades later, when I realized it was supposed to be "out of the frying pan, into the fire," which meant things were going from bad to worse. I wonder how many things she thought were getting worse, but I translated as, *Oh, good, she's baking.*

Misquoting old sayings often reveals a deeper truth we didn't intend to share. For example, the stress of COVID-19 crawling through the country, with staggering numbers as the months wore on, was waking us up to the truth that people can't breathe. Not only in the Black Lives Matter protests, but everyone stuck behind the stale air of their masks. That reality was hitting survivors of trauma hard at Thistle Farms. Not only had some of the women I served been gagged and had hands held over their mouths, but unspoken cultural insensitivity and bias were seeping through cracks we had taped over with platitudes.

When I tried to tell a friend that traumatic events unfolding at work, including a whole department getting COVID-19 and screaming fights, weren't getting to me, I said, "It's like a duck on water." When she laughed, I realized I'd meant to say, "It's like water off a duck's back." But the truth was what I'd actually said. I was going under.

Sometimes, no matter how much we hate to admit it, when we want it to be like *water off a duck's back*, it is more like *a duck on water*. We are waist deep in it.

I have been waist deep for decades, but 2020 pulled us all deeper into the water. This year has made me rant. It has made me go back and examine my past that, in truth, doesn't contain just one predator, but five. For decades I only focused on the first, yet somehow, confronting the grandson, then moving into lockdown, made me want to piece together the larger story that is all too common for young women: once there is sexual abuse, a lot more comes on its heels.

So, this whole thing feels like a duck on water. And I am paddling to stay afloat. There are valuable lessons, though, as we paddle our way through. In the midst of it, it feels like the world is throwing open the doors to old assumptions, statutes, and myths, and we're all discovering new practically divine truths. We have permission to cull the meaning of old sayings and stories and then toss out the rest, like racist mascots of old football teams and Twitter trolls. The expression "come to find out" is expansive and means we have made a realization. It also infers that oftentimes truth comes as a surprise.

Who knew the system was rigged? is a thought that might one day dawn on us in mid-protest.

You mean to tell me that, when I was abused and then ran outside to play, the event I'd just endured wasn't over?, we might muse as a therapist sheds light on why we flinch when a man hugs us in greeting.

Sometimes when we "come to find out," it feels as dramatic, yet subtle, as being "knocked over with a feather." The reality is that we have probably been touched by a thousand feathers landing all around us, offering glimpses into a new understanding, until one lands in the exact right place at the exact right moment, and we think, *Ah, yes—now I see it.* When we "come to find out" truths that people buried in shallow graves. Our practical work is to uncover and try to restore the untarnished truth lying beneath.

I have never heard a more powerful story about the hard work of uncovering the truth in a big pile of rubbish than I did from Teena.

Teena, a Thistle Farms graduate, was raised in a rural religious cult. She was taught that God was a harsh God, a God of hail, fire, and brimstone. She was never told that God was love. In her life, she'd encountered several people like the church elder from my youth, who'd twisted the sickness of their own power and need into a religion meant to keep you quiet at all costs. When I asked Teena to explain, she wrote:

I was taught that everything I did would damn me to hell. Girls were to wear long dresses to their ankles, sleeves to their wrists, and buns on top of their heads. No part of our bodies could show that was worldly, or we would be thrown into the lake of fire. In reality, the cult was a cesspool of pedophiles who had their pick of child brides. One perpetrator after another became normal to me, because it was being taught in the name of God behind the pulpit of the religious cult where I was being raised.

For thirty-two years, it defined my path. I became a victim of trafficking, prostitution, promiscuity, heroin addiction, nameless other addictions, depression, oppression, hopelessness. I was on sinking sand; I was in darkness with no light at the end of the tunnel. I had overdosed more times than I could count, and each time, somehow, in some way, I came out of it. I didn't understand. I woke up every day mad at the only harsh God I knew. Why wouldn't He just let me die?

When I came to Thistle Farms, I was so broken—I thought I was beyond repair. I didn't believe the concept that "love heals everybody." How could it? I never knew love to give love. As time has passed, something inside of me has awakened. It's something I can't explain.

Teena had come to find out that the deep and brutal lessons she was taught weren't the truth, and she could claim something else. She could live a more practically divine life by shaking off old lies and stepping into the freeing truth, where she could thrive. She said she is "overwhelmingly drawn to the concept now that maybe, just maybe, love truly does heal everybody, even a worldly sinner like me. In all my brokenness, I will be made whole. And I can't help but believe it was love that led me here."

We are allowed to speak our truth about God without fear of reprisal, and when old, worn-out tactics to keep us fearful don't help you, shake them off.

One day I saw Teena in her job at the café at Thistle Farms, standing with all her coworkers and sister survivors, singing "Happy Birthday" to a customer. The café has a different version of the birthday song, with fun clapping in syncopated rhythms. She was singing, clapping, and laughing, and I wondered if her freedom and joy came in a whirlwind carrying a feather, which floated on a graceful thought that landed and finally gave her permission to be herself.

• • •

IT'S WORTH REVISITING old sayings, like old assumptions, that were instilled in us, to see what we need to dismantle and dismiss, to find new truth. In the work of the practically divine, it's a good time for us to come to find out. Like protests that call for dismantling old, racist systems, rethinking the rote learnings of our past may help us figure out how we got here and help us make some *practical changes*.

I can hear the remnants of harmful myths in old sayings that need to be parsed out and discarded, so we don't keep myths alive that perpetuate hatred and fear. Language is important, and as much as we wish some of the old sayings and myths weren't in our heads, they are. For instance, why is an old racist chant from my third-grade experience, of being bused in the south to integrate schools, still in my head forty years later? Why do I still say, "killing two birds with one stone," when it's so violent? I heard someone say, fairly casually, that I conducted worship for the "peanut gallery." Yeah, it's pretty racist and ridiculous as it refers to the cheapest seats reserved for black patrons during vaudeville's heyday.

We repeat old stuff we heard that wasn't helpful to us when we first heard it. We aren't crazy—we just need to sort through the memory storage unit, then discern and distill treasures from rubble. We still have racist, violent children's songs in our collective memory bank. They were placed there by folks who showed us how to play "German spotlight," the tag game in the dark mimicking the hunt for Jews by Nazis, or chant "smear the queer" as a group tackled whoever was holding the ball. These types of sayings and songs are like some of the old junk I have stashed in the garage space of my heart. We all have stuff inside of us that needs to be discarded. Then we can have space to "come to find out" and live more practically divine.

Much poetry is born by picking apart pithy aphorisms to see what truth lies inside. Blurring the lines between the poetic and pragmatic is a practically divine exercise that helps us see the depth of words and deeds that live in between. The goal in pulling apart old sayings is to ascribe more precise language to reveal deeper truth. Old sayings make references to plagues long since forgotten and oppression buried beneath monuments. "Ring Around the Rosie" is a rhyme about the plague that is still sung by children four hundred years later. Sayings still around, like "sold down the river," might mean you are being cheated, but it also has deep roots in slavery.

Sayings, no matter how poetic or memorable, can be imprecise and fail to account for people's original experiences. The other day, an Irish friend and I were walking and talking about old expressions of our mothers. We laughed when she remembered her mother's words, "That is a cry waiting for a slap." Then I wanted to weep. The saying is funny, and it offers a heartbreaking truth when you parse the way an eight-year-old child hears it from a towering figure with hands bigger than the child's face. Much is left for us to "come to find out" as we separate the wheat and the chaff of our pasts. Realization is a divine gift that comes as we see practically that things are not as we imagined or were taught. We're allowed to keep learning new lessons and keep coming to find out. Loving the world doesn't mean we have to change it. It means that we have to be willing to change to love it better.

Nowhere is this more apparent to me than in parenting. As soon as we think we've got it, everything changes, and we have to come to find out all over again. An easy example is how we have to keep learning how to feed our children, one of the most basic things we're supposed to do. When a friend's mother saw me feeding my baby, she said, "Ooh, they have a million loaves to eat." But fairly quickly, kids grow and feed themselves. The way we feed twenty-year-olds versus two-year-olds is completely different, and we must be willing to change in order to feed them well.

That truth can be applied across the board: to keep finding out, we have to keep changing.

* * *

WITHIN A COUPLE years of starting my first nonprofit, it dawned on me that I needed a new set of skills. When I figured out that leadership meant I needed to step out of management, it was hard—"when your child walks out the door for college" hard. If I was going to help launch survivor artisan groups around the world, I had to let go of the day-to-day work in Nashville.

One day, I walked into our community and there was a directors' meeting, and I hadn't been invited. At first it felt like I'd caught a lover cheating on me! "What the hell is going on in here?" I could have screamed. Come to find out, they were fine without me. In fact, better. I needed to learn the dance of the deep bow of gratitude and backing up with grace.

While love is changeless, *how* we love changes all the time. In other words, I love my husband and children, period. But how I love them and how I show them that I love them have changed over time. Even in love we come to find out. Come to find out is healthy, and we could all use a bit of it as we grow in love in our lives. If you are not willing to change, you are not willing to love.

My sister says people are willing to change when staying the same is more painful. Changing doesn't mean simply doing something differently. Changing involves a willing spirit, a new thought, and plenty of backbone. Changing can mean sloughing off our past like an old skin, so old stories no longer define us. And some of those old stories were written for us before we even knew how to write. We can determine the truth or lies that wrote those old stories. We can close the chapter on the stories that don't help us anymore. Experiencing the freedom of new understanding and knowledge makes the past bearable, and sometimes we can even celebrate its lessons.

Kristina, one of the women I get to work with daily at Thistle Farms, talks about the great change in her life when she closed a chapter and began to write a new story. When she and her sister were children, they were in a tragic accident. Her sister died, and the mythical story Kristina lived in, which didn't allow her to change, was that she didn't deserve to live, and she wished her sister had lived instead. Such a story led her to horrible abuse and addiction, which landed her in the hospital at age twenty-two, with a damaged heart that would require opening her chest. She came out of the experience changed. She knew she had to do more than change what she was doing—she needed to change her past story to heal her heart. It was heroic work, and some three years later, seeing her come to find out has been inspiring for thousands of women.

Kristina has appeared twice with me on *The Kelly Clarkson Show*, the first time as a surprise guest to thank me for what I had done. My reaction on the show was a surprise to me. I didn't feel like crying, and I wasn't embarrassed. My reaction with what I hope was unaffected feeling: "Y'all have no idea." Y'all have no idea who is sitting on this couch thanking me. This brilliant young woman almost died twice, and we are all going to come to find out she is the strongest one sitting here on the Kelly Clarkson couch. All I did in that moment was thank Kristina, a strong, twenty-five-year-old woman, who has come to find out the truth that love is powerful enough to overcome the past, shame, fear, and depression. I told

Kelly and the studio audience that I believe Kristina is just getting started. She has dreams she hasn't even thought of yet, and my prayer is that she can continue to help people come to find out more about what is possible when you're willing to change your life.

•   •   •

THERE IS NOTHING like truth coming in and knocking down an old myth we have been sheltered under. We have come to find out that amid the hard and holy fields of sickness and economic hardships caused by the pandemic, good things are revealed that free us and connect us to one another. You never read about that in the history of past pandemics. As families were huddled inside against a plague, they were probably telling stories and playing cards. They probably saw close ties between economics and health and deemed frontline workers heroic, just like we have. I bet they also composed and created things, like we are doing to make it through, and discovered hidden talents and poetic leanings. Having lived through this shared experience, where the whole world is rethinking holidays, I can imagine with more ease how a mom a thousand years ago adapted traditions to fit her family. I can feel the hope of a new year dawning, as they may have done a hundred years ago with the last pandemic.

As we've been living through this pandemic, it's easier to imagine how and why children's songs were written the way they were. Previously, I thought it was macabre, but now I'm thinking, *Good for you.* When you're staring at months ahead with no relief, and you still have the energy to create a game for kids, I applaud it. Now that we're older and wiser from the pandemic, the goal is to glean all the lessons and forge a new path, not just slip back into the way it was.

•   •   •

I HAVE COME to find out pandemics get us to the essentials of what we love and believe fairly quickly—a pandemic can clear social clutter by social distancing, and we sort through our thoughts and deeds with more precision as the world shutters. Pandemics provide the time to slow cook, as well as slow read and slow think. The pandemic of 2020 and beyond was our time to learn how the practically divine is carrying the day. We could feel the old injustices that had been buried in shallow graves come to life. The women in unsafe homes pleading for help. The prisoners and refugees being unjustly exposed. People who were economically vulnerable were being exposed at a higher rate. All this old truth was surfacing as we were all coming to find out. They were not new injustices, but freshly uncovered, which shed new light to the old injustices.

If we want to come to find out, we need to see the practically divine at work in hard times like pandemics, as well as sweeter seasons like golden ages. The practically divine teaches us that now, whenever *now* is, is an extraordinary time, and this, wherever *this* is, is an extraordinary place where we can come to find out where love lives.

*   *   *

TO EXPERIENCE SUCH extraordinariness is a matter of learning to pivot from having sight to beholding a vision in the blink of an eye. Having vision is practically divine. To have vision does not require gazing into a crystal ball to predict a new thing or to see the future. Thank God all we need to do is love the world and be willing to see the truth of it to love it more. We only need to look again and allow our sight to be full of imagination and grace.

After months of social distancing, millions of us were at home, cleaning out old closets and drawers we had ignored. I found, tucked into the corner of an old drawer, a hand-sized, dusty prayer book, inscribed in 1941 to Jean Hummon, the mother of my husband, Marcus, by her pastor. It said "private use" on the cover. It was like a Spark-Notes version of the *Book of Common Prayer*, and it felt intimate, as it could fit in the palm of your hand.

My first feeling was surprise that my now deceased mother-in-law had a small prayer book. In the thirty years I'd known her, I'd never heard her mention using a prayer book. But it must have meant something for her to keep it. She had endured some trauma as a child, and maybe this book was like a security blanket for her as she wound her way through some pretty shadowy valleys.

Within a few minutes of finding the book and leafing through it, it moved from a sweet memory to something holy. Under the initial inscription, I saw that in 1974, my husband's mom signed it with love to him, when he was a teenager. She must have wanted him to be safe. I can see her passing it to him with little fanfare or notice. Maybe she knew he needed that security when he was going through some of his own valleys.

I don't know that he even remembers he has the book. And I have no idea how it ended up in this drawer of mine. But what I did know instinctively, like I know when the temperature is perfect for the larkspur to bloom, was that it was a moment to stop, let what I was seeing sink deeper, and understand not only the tenderness of this book but also what I needed to learn from it.

I'd never seen it until this pandemic and, somehow, because it had been hiding for decades and was small and well-used, finding it felt sacred. The prayers had had time to germinate and take root. This miniature prayer book had survived World War II and could carry my family through. I wondered if it was time for my husband to sign over the book to our youngest son, who had been sent home from college and was wondering what to do.

For now, I just needed to see it, hold it, and take it in.

In that tiny prayer book, I could feel security and grounding, two things I didn't even know I was needing to get on with my work and love the world. Security—I needed to feel safe from sickness. Grounding—I needed to know I could stand on all that I have worked for, and it wouldn't collapse under me.

When I left the room, holding the book in my closed hand, there was a healing. I didn't take a class or search the world. I just saw what was before me on that ordinary day in those extraordinary times. Then I stayed with the sight long enough for it to become a vision and teach me what I needed to learn. I looked at the tiny, dusty book and allowed what I was seeing to sink in deep enough to become a vision of something holy, like a relic. I was in the presence of amazing grace for long enough to feel found and grounded. Through the toils and snares, sitting and reading a prayer that I imagined got a mother through a night of bombing in England some seventy years ago, I felt safe and ready to meet my day with a fresh spirit. The miracle of vision is allowing yourself to see with something deeper than your eyes.

Visions can be old and as simple as considering birds and grass again. Most vision comes from within—the gift is looking at something before us and finally *seeing* it. Seeing how extraordinary it is, seeing how sacred it feels, and seeing how it fills us with vision. There is a cost to vision, a freedom in vision, and culpability in vision. It means we can't unsee, and it means we lose the veil of ignorance. But what a sad thing it would be not to allow ourselves the gift of seeing with vision. We would miss the low-flying hawks that whisper inspiration into our hearts. We would miss the spiraling of the incense that encourages us to pray. We would miss the dragons in the clouds that dance us into bravery.

I feel like I can feel the transformation of sight into vision more easily when I feel the presence of salty prisms of gratitude, mixed in for good measure. We are all graced with vision. Our job is to practice seeing the sacred in the ordinary all around us. I am coming to find out that the more I can see what lies before me and let go of old sayings and assumptions that have not served me or the world well, the more I can change.

•   •   •

THE KNOWLEDGE THAT we can change is the best news of "come to find out." We can be free from the binds of lies or prejudices we've been told. We can be free from our past and close the chapter on old stories. We don't have to experience whiplash from following conflicting opinions telling us what it means to be faithful or how to be a good citizen. We can see, we can change, we can have vision. We can discover and learn new things.

Another important way we come to find out is by listening to stories. As I've been working alongside survivor leaders for almost thirty years, taking in all the anecdotal truths they're teaching, I have learned volumes about common-sense justice. Instead of only reading theoretical reports that make us feel inadequate and unworthy of a thought, we listen to one another, share stories, and keep working as we figure it out. I didn't know opening a

house would lead to a global movement for women's freedom. But I did know that, if I opened a house, I could learn
and listen alongside women who could build something
beautiful.

Jennifer Clinger, a great survivor leader, published
her memoir and created a concert about her life with two
musicians. On stage she shares her story and they sing
songs, hoping to help other women and girls "come to
find out." She says her desire is to help us all understand
the myths and truths about why women are on the streets
and what it takes for women to find their way to freedom.
Her story challenges anyone who says old, ridiculous
things such as "world's oldest profession" or "She made
some bad choices." After hearing her story, any reasonable person would question whether any of her story was
her "choice."

Jennifer was thirteen years old when she stood on the
entrance ramp of Interstate 70 in Dayton, Ohio, hoping to
escape her life. In minutes, a semi driver picked her up. She
was in luck, he said. He would take care of her and show
her the world. Instead, after assaulting her, he proceeded
to call other truckers: "I have a sweet young thing here
who's heading out to Los Angeles. If you take care of her,
she will take care of you." Jennifer was delivered to the
next truck and soon after was exploited by traffickers
across the country. Her life was marked by ongoing assault,
child pornography, addiction, prostitution, and violence.

The sexual abuse had begun when she was just a few
years old. She isn't sure when, but she remembers a crib,

and that it continued for years. After a childhood spent acting out, she was deemed a troublemaker. She married at seventeen and had some beautiful babies. But the relationship was abusive, and when she lost a child in childbirth, the wave of buried pain sitting below the surface washed up, and she was gone.

I met Jennifer after she walked into a Catholic church in Ohio, and the priest gave her the number for Thistle Farms. I love the creative, funny, and passionate parts of Jennifer that still inspire me ten years later. I respect her brilliance and ability to claim the ground she stands on.

It was hard for me to imagine the day before she walked into that church. The day sitting on a hillside beside a bridge and thinking about killing herself. She said she was so tired and broken, and that the only thing that kept her going was a thread of truth she remembered that God loved her. There were lots of other threads. She says that, looking back, she could see the common thread woven into the story of exploitation: the men who trafficked her knew everything they needed to know.

"It's a secret club with their own codes," she said. "They have an understanding of the ins and outs of child sexual assault. I have since learned that young children who are scared and alone become immediate targets for human traffickers, child pornographers, and pedophiles."

I have come to find out so much through the teaching of Jennifer and many of her sisters. I have come to find out that there is no such thing as teenage prostitutes, only adolescents who have been trafficked. I have come to find out that the connection between war and trafficking is real, especially for the most vulnerable women and refugees. I have come to find out that the social constructs of poverty create the violence and vulnerability necessary for the trafficking of human beings.

I could go on, but I believe that more than three statements is considered a rant. I'll just add one more for good measure: I have come to find out that alcohol and drugs are some of the first medications many of the women I work with used to numb traumatic experiences.

•   •   •

"COME TO FIND out" realizations are practically divine thoughts as ephemeral and fickle as muses. I covet new thoughts to discover new meaning. A thought can slip out of reach between breaths. It can rise with such promise, then dissipate on a wisp of a cloud. That is why we spend so much time having to rethink. *What was the original thought?* Having a thought isn't like discovering a new country—it's more like rediscovering an old country for the first time.

I have lost so much thought content through committees, where it feels like the muse goes to die. It feels like the activity I partake in weekly, when I'm walking up the stairs to fetch something and get distracted while I'm walking up, so when I arrive at the top of the staircase, I can't remember why I went. Then I go back down and put myself back into the place I was when I first decided I needed to go upstairs to retrieve something. "Oh, yes," I say to myself, and plod back up.

That is how it is with thoughts. We have a thought that needs another thought, but in chasing the next thought, we get distracted along the way and can't remember why we needed to think about this other thing. So, we have to go back to the original thought.

Yes, I remember: I was thinking about the search for inspired thought.

Several years ago, I was sitting on a bench in Ecuador, sharing a cup of tea with a friend who lives in Mexico. He started telling me about a small group of women who could grow moringa for tea, and he wanted to help. He asked me if I was interested. With just a simple thought rising about how we could blend love, tea, and support strong women, I said yes. It is a rare and precious gift to get a thought that transforms into a vague vision sitting on steps anywhere, and I didn't want it to leave me before I acted.

That thought lead to taking several trips to the mountains of Mexico, to starting a company, and to developing new brands and tea collections. We've gotten distracted many times, and at the end of the day, when we're overwhelmed by shipping and packaging, it's good to remember: *Ah, yes—this was about love.*

When you have a thought, seize the day. Shellac the damn thing if you need to. It is the truest form of practically divine. Take that thought and study it from all angles. Where did it come from? What is the thought's backstory?

Was it a dream? Did it arise with a visual? Did it secretly live in you for decades, like a brown recluse in a basement? Where does the thought carry you? Who can you trust this thought treasure? A thought is precious, and you know you paid a great value for it, so you can't let it be tossed to swine.

Be alert to your thought and wait. Thoughts generally don't travel alone; they are like pack animals. They arrive with brother and sister thoughts that want to dine together. They come and, if they find a place to nest, they will stay with you, put down roots, and start to grow. It is a wondrous truth that the power of thought is the greatest and cannot be leashed or killed. Thank you, God, there are no thought police. Thoughts roam free in this world, and they are your very own.

In Ralph Waldo Emerson's essay on self-reliance, he said that what defines true genius is one's ability to cultivate original thought. Every revolution started with a thought from one person. When we have a thought and cultivate it and share it with other people who have similar thoughts, and the thoughts change and take on more weight, a movement can be born. I remember growing into my adulthood as the world was coming to find out about AIDS. One of the most powerful ways of combating the fears and myths came as family and friends sewed a quilt that took over the National Mall in Washington, DC. Each three-foot quilt square told the life story of someone who had died of AIDS. The rich quilted squares allowed people from all over the world to grieve the formerly anonymous names. Now there were beautiful squares depicting funny, talented, and beautiful people beloved by many. It took the scary issue and turned it into a human issue we could all work on together. I can imagine one mom grieving her son and thinking, *I think I want to quilt this*, one thought leading to the birth of the largest quilt humanity has ever seen.

• • •

SEVERAL OF THE organizations I've founded have one thing in common: when I tell their origin story, they begin with the line, "I was walking in the woods." That is the place where I can think a thought. The woods are a place where thoughts are free to roam and then take root. I will gladly fly halfway around the world or walk for days for a new thought that yields a poem. I feel my money is well spent if I buy a book and read it for days and, halfway through, a single sentence sparks something in my soul and a new idea arises. That brings me as much joy as ocean sunsets and wildflower mountains. It is that bright and beautiful. And it lives in all of us.

We have everything we need to raise a thought. The same thought can rise in many people, but when it rises in you, it is your thought, and you can take it where you want. Through its caterpillar stage, it can grow inside you. When it builds a chrysalis—God willing and the creek don't rise—no one tears it down and it's given the time and space it needs to sprout wings. Then sometime, usually after more time than you'd planned and after more money than you'd budgeted, your thought can fly off with friends in spectacular beauty, in the form of a butterfly.

To believe our own thoughts and see that they might be true for others is what genius philosophers, poets, priests, and politicians have cultivated. Such thoughts lie waiting for discovery in our souls and call us to pay attention to our own inklings. To recognize the gleam of light that flashes before us when a new thought breaks the hard ground of our cynicism, fear, ignorance, or laziness. There is no need for envy or imitation; this is the place to simply recognize your own true thoughts and find the space and freedom to explore them. Think of our inner selves as one of the former homes that sometimes appears in our dreams. Inevitably in those dreams, you discover unexpected rooms and vast staircases you've never traveled down before. That is what it's like to search the chasm of that infinite space between our heads and our hearts and stir up the soul for rich thought.

Some of the best kinds of thoughts are called *whims*. Whims are particularly practically divine in that they are like a dare. They say, "Follow me and see what you come to find out." They seem fanciful and dreamy, less a theorem and more a poem. Whims start us on journeys and get us to step onto new land. A whim is like a hope that we can come to find out. You know where you have been, you can feel where you are now, and then step out and learn something new.

⬢　⬢　⬢

THIS IDEA OF stepping onto new ground on a whim or with new thoughts is especially important in cultivating faith. If the story of faith that you grew up with doesn't work for you anymore, if the God you have proclaimed has grown too small for all the wisdom you have gleaned from the crumbs you have collected, you can change. My mom often would say, "You are free to believe what you want." In some ways, she probably meant that, since I disagreed with her, even though I was dead wrong, I was free to think that way and see where it got me. But she was so right. We are free to believe what we want. That is a God-given right that is practical and divine. This is the only way to know what we can discover. We are free to come to find out. I have learned that over and over from patient teachers like Teena, Kristina, and Jennifer. I believe stories can uncover the most dramatic come-to-find-out truths.

⬢　⬢　⬢

ONCE, I SAT with a woman who had been in solitary confinement for most of her twenties. She was in a five-by-ten-foot cell for all the years that most of us were establishing careers and falling in love a few times. When I asked her how she'd survived, she said, "I was in prison a lot longer than that. Since I was little, I have been isolated and abused. This is my first experience ever in freedom. I had to discard the lies, find a God of my own understanding, and decide I wanted to live."

The recipe for come-to-find-out moments calls for equal amounts of preparation and surprise blended with practice and a dash of luck. This recipe was served with perfection to millions of people during the solar eclipse on August 21, 2017. The moments came on a platter that day, as people planned and prepared with amazing glasses and careful spaces for viewing. But you couldn't plan the insights into the universe and your soul as the moon blocked out the sun, and shadows became misshapen and danced like water. I am so grateful for all the scientists who have spent careers looking into the sky and telling us all to get ready, or I may well have been staring at a screen as I learned that even a sliver of sun can light the world in dreamy wonder.

When the moon finally blocked the sun, I was surprised how I felt, for the briefest second, the infinity of forgiveness. There before me, it looked like the universe had been wiped clean, and I could imagine how forgiveness never ends. As the moon swept the sun for a minute in darkness, and then that light sparkled and reached across the world, it felt like the whole slate was wiped clean. We may not get it, we may not get there, but it is all forgiven. In the fullness of time, it's all forgiven. It was an amazing feeling. We can love and forgive everything. And I am sure that as wondrous and freeing as that moment was, it doesn't begin to touch the truth and depth of God's forgiveness, and I have a lifetime more of preparation and surprise ahead of me as I come to find out more.

Preparation and surprise blend into divine insight that doesn't hand us truth but offers us enough to keep on a search that will last us our whole lives. I get worried in this world when we proclaim we have *the truth*. As though since we have discovered the truth, we need no more insights or changes in our lives. I always think back to what my brother says: "Almost the truth is still a lie." If we can avoid holding on to the truth like it's a wad of bills in our fist, we can hold on to new, refreshing insights. If we can stay humble enough to know we do not possess the ability to hold all history and truth in our heads, we will be regarded as worthy to be gifted with new knowledge.

When the eclipse ended, I wanted to jump for joy at the overwhelming feeling of glimpsing into the power of forgiveness. It only took about an hour, on the drive back into town, for that feeling to dissipate into the traffic and worries about the next day.

Sometimes I think we are about halfway to the truth. We see signs along the way, but we still have a long way to go. You are not there yet; I am not there yet. But we have caught some glimpses in signs and stories left like bread crumbs along the way. Keep following them, planning and being open to surprising moments when you once again are graced to come to find out.

NO WORDS

When no words come

I hold my pencil to the paper

Hoping some inspired muse will happen by

Guiding my hesitant graphite strokes

To unveil a truth I didn't know lived in me.

No one can do this work for me.

I have to sit and look beyond my horizon toward

What lives beyond my vision.

If I wait for the perfect moment,

The page will stay blank,

The time will pass

And the pencil and I

Will return to our common end.

The desires of my heart will not fertilize the

Yolk of my deepest longings.

The revolution of thought will lie dormant

Inside the numbing drone of my daily tasks.

The genius of creativity will wilt in the

Dry beds of my acquiescence.

So I will begin and write a single word—

And call it blessed.

| FIVE |

Bound to Grace

IN THE PREVIOUS CHAPTERS, we delved into the topics of vision, creativity, and discovery as essential work in living practically divine. Visioning, creating, and discovering are gifts descending like sweet sunlight that shines on us all. We didn't do anything to deserve such gifts, and the only thing we can do is bask in their descending rays. They shine on the just and the unjust, thank God. In such light, dappled by trees that keep us alive, filled with dancing leaves in wind that embraces our skin, we'd be remiss to forget the ever-present truth that "life is a gift." It is more than mercy that is twice blessed.

Life is the experience of waking up every day bound to a loving Creator who offers us new breath each morning. No matter where we find ourselves, we can rest assured we are not lost—we are bound to grace. We can be in a prison, in a refugee camp, in an unhappy marriage, or at the end of a road, yet still we are bound to grace. In living practically divine, no matter where we are or how intensely we feel joy or grief, we are in a state of grace. Social distancing, injustice, and our own inadequacies cannot loosen us.

Being in a state of grace can be hard to remember with all the things pushing and pulling at us. So, claiming we are "bound to grace" is the most divine truth we know. Grace—that beautiful, ephemeral aspect of the divine that fills in all the spaces where we feel less than or unworthy.

When we are bound to grace, it also means we are tied inextricably to love. It means there is something unchanging in the stunning changes and chances all around us, as our lives unfold. On one of the hardest days I can recall in my adult life, in the midst of the chaos, I remember that there was a steady presence of love.

A friend of mine, a dermatologist, wanted to give me the gift of a chemical peel. About twenty-four hours later, I was sitting on my back porch and beginning to feel the burn of the peel, as my reddened skin began to shed like a flimsy snakeskin. I was joking about it with another friend sitting there, as I planned a birthday party for my youngest son.

While we were sitting on the porch and laughing, my brother-in-law called, crying. My sister had had an aneurysm and died. She had been fine that morning and started feeling sick and then collapsed and died. And just like that, I went from planning a party to planning a funeral and writing the eulogy for my sister.

Within twenty-four hours, everyone in my family was gathered in my living room, as we sorted through old photos and told stories. My chemical peel was now in full swing, with salty tears burning furrows down my cheeks. I ended up packing tissue paper around sunglasses to stop the burning. My other siblings and I sat for hours in my living room, grieving at the unexpected loss, but grounding ourselves in memory and in our close proximity to one another. They gave me a lot of grief about my chemical peel, and I have never been more humiliated, preaching with skin flying off my face. But somehow, that stupid chemical peel brought us joy in the midst of grief, laughter in the midst of tears, and I could feel grace remembering the truth that even in death we are bound to love.

On the opposite side, I also know things that seem overwhelming and bad can change fairly quickly. Flimsy relationships, like the one I started with the grandson I wrote about at the beginning of the book, have scattered like the wind. When there is no public worship, my proximity to people I don't know is gone. Getting some much-needed space because of a global pandemic held grace as well as grief.

As I'm writing, I wonder what will happen to the thread of this story with the grandson. I hope he is well and safe, and I am grateful for all the grace the pandemic offered.

Being unbound by the rigors of my travel, preaching, and teaching freed me to let go of the stuff that kept me binded, not bound. I'm not pretending there won't be something else down the road. But today, just for today, I can feel that the months of being separated from 95 percent of my community holds some gift. The hope for all of us is that we learn from what we have endured and never let the graceful lessons slip between our schedules as they fill up in our return.

In the residential community, for months and months, women have experienced the same thing. The families and relationships that caused old traumas to stir new drama have been removed. There is a peace that passes understanding in the fact that, as old triggers are removed, we can feel grace more expediently. So many people had no idea there were so many things to worry about before the pandemic. And so many other things that we worried about before have disappeared and opened us to a more present grace.

I had seriously worried about jet lag from a speaking gig I was doing in Australia before flying directly to lead a group in Peru. As it turned out, I was in the same time zone for more than a year, and that silly fear vanished faster than supplies on shelves. The world keeps shifting, as it always has, and to live in the present means finding the constant that is practically divine.

Of all the practical and divine mom phrases, this idea that we are "bound to grace" carried me through some of the times I have been most lost in my work, in my family, and in my faith. If we can only remember that we are loved, we can get through the longest nights followed by longer days. It is why the motto for Thistle Farms is simply "love heals." That is what grounds us and defines our work. It surpasses understanding, so the goal isn't to have someone try to explain that truth.

You are loved, my mom would say, "bound to grace." She may well have said, "Because I told you so," when I inevitably asked, "Why?" Explaining how we are bound to grace is like trying to explain how an infinite universe is expanding. If it's infinite, how is there room to grow? If it's expanding, what was there before? I am grateful for truths that don't require my understanding and are simply woven into the fabric of creation. I don't understand the vast expanse of interstellar space, the planets in their courses, or even this fragile island where life thrives. "Bound to grace" is not a sentence to parse—it is an idea to let root around in your chest, then sprout into practically divine ideas as you experience it.

* * *

OF ALL THE questions I get as a pastor, the most authentic is, "What happens when I die?" The practically divine answer is that we are angels and dirt, simply bound to grace. No one knows what it means that everything but love dies. No one needs to explain how it is that signs and dreams are prevalent after the death of someone we love. No one without a deep love for metaphor can describe heaven, which my mom used to say is the memory of God. Being bound to grace means that the essence of who we are—love—doesn't disappear when we die.

And for those of us who have been grieving since we were children, we can live with being inextricably bound to grace. We can let go of our need to try to understand, and grasp the freedom of being bound to love infinitely.

When my brother-in-law, John Westman's, mom died, he said, "Can I have a conversation with you about the afterlife?"

I told him, "Of course, but I don't have much to say, since I have never experienced it." We laughed, and the conversation slid into how our kids were doing and the sad state of politics.

Months later he called and asked if we could still have that conversation about what happens after we die.

"Sure," I said, "but I don't have much to say, since I have never been." We laughed again, but of course it was only funny that I repeated myself, not that I kept putting him off. So, I stopped myself from doing the thing I do, which is act busy and change subjects, and I said, "Tell me what you think."

What ensued was a conversation about the deep bond and longing between mothers and sons, and how he hopes that these are reflected in the deep bond between humanity and divinity. The most important thing I could do was not have an answer, but honor the bond already there. He didn't need me to explain why he missed his mom or any details about heaven. He needed me to honor that he didn't believe that even death could break that bond.

I believe in that bond. When I became a mom, I spent hours and hours beholding our firstborn son. I could count the hairs on his head. I could describe the soft peach fuzz above his right ear and the way his left ear was a tiny bit different. I knew the way his cheek moved when he started to drift off to sleep, and when the first freckle emerged on his neck. I knew him like no other in this world, and there was an unbreakable bond between us. That bond feels similar to God beholding each of us like a child, knowing us before we say a word, before we know anything about ourselves. We have been searched out and known, loved, and claimed.

* * *

WHEN WE THINK the bond between us and the eternal—or even the bonds that connect us as humanity—are broken, it leaves us feeling like we're traversing uncharted, stormy seas, trying to hold on to our anger and grief on one side, and then hope and joy on the other, as counterbalances. But our deepest bonds aren't broken by death or circumstances. The early saints said the words that best summarize the truth that we are bound to grace: "For I am convinced that neither death, nor life, nor angels, nor rulers, nor things present, nor things to come, nor powers, nor height, nor depth, nor anything else in all

creation, will be able to separate us from the love of God"
(Romans 8:38–39).

We are bound to grace first because we are made in the
image of God and begin our lives with original grace. It
was there from the start. Our lives all start and end with
God, and we are worthy of all good things. We never need
to live in shame for all the things that have been done to us,
that we have done to others, or that have been left undone.
There are times in history and in our lives when we might
swear the bond has been severed, when we instead feel
bound to old injustices and prejudices.

The shame I have carried for the stupid and selfish
things I have done over the years is a strong force in my
life. I am my mother's daughter, and I know there is some
motivation in guilt. But I am firmly in the camp that grace
is the real motivator, as it signals, "You are free." We don't
have to keep everything balanced or hold on to anything.
All we have to do is remember that we are bound to grace.
That means we surrender everything else, and we're free
to love with divine practicality that is sustainable and
scalable.

Last weekend, I stood in the simple chapel where I
serve as chaplain, with six people for Gwen's wedding.
Gwen, like many of the women I serve in the Thistle
Farms community, knew sexual assault and drugs before
she knew how to locate herself on a map. In one of her
more tragic stories, she describes how she and her sister
shared a room where some of her earliest memories of
trauma took root. She is the definition of a survivor leader

and has raised her children and helped train hundreds of women working at Thistle Farms. She speaks her mind and doesn't "suffer fools gladly," as my mom would say. She came into the residential community of Thistle Farms fifteen years ago without "two pennies to rub together," and I felt like we knew each other pretty well.

In the midst of the pandemic, economic hardship, and cries from around the country that "I can't breathe," she was trying to plan a wedding, and she was mad. She was furious about what she felt was unstated racism within the community, about her family, and about money. She said to me, "I know you want me to be grateful, but I'm not—I am mad as hell." She was as angry as women I have known over the years who thank their rapists for driving them back into town instead of leaving them on some remote roadside. Months later, the rage they should have directed at their attacker emerges and turns small issues into huge arguments. They are finally and rightfully angry as hell. Anger can feel like an explosion that can destroy relationships and community. But, seriously, anger is just surface stuff. There is so much underneath it, and if you can find a way together to get to that, it is powerful and life-changing. Remember that the next time you want to blow! What hell is underneath this powerful feeling? And the next time someone yells at you, for just the next breath, stop and remember: this is where the deep soil lives.

I am convinced that the reason I remained married to Marcus for more than thirty years is that he stuck with me during my deepest angers. On the very first night I slept at his home, I elbowed him in the face while we were both asleep. I was dreaming he was slapping me in the face, and I lashed out. At that point, he must have had a clue that I had some triggers. He never retaliated with anger to my lashing out, whether awake or asleep. He knew it was stuff I had to get through to get better.

There is plenty to be angry about in this world, and there are plenty of reasons to step away from one another. But there is freedom if we can stay bound to one another in grace.

I showed up at the chapel before the ceremony as Gwen and her maid of honor were in the back room, trying to lace up her dress. A silk ribbon about twenty-five feet long had to be threaded down her back and tucked into a bustle. There was no way for one person to do it alone, so I joined them. We had to push against her and lean into her to get the ribbon tight between the lacing. Finally, there was no way to continue tightening this external corset without kneeling down before her. We all started laughing as we pulled and tucked and pulled and tucked everything into place. That laughter was the grace that pulled us back together, like the bound dress. Minutes later, she walked down the aisle through an empty church. I snapped a photo as soon as the ceremony ended, and Gwen was bathed in a bright beam of light. She was radiant as she had made her promise to love. We are both the broken and the healer, bound to one another in a moment of grace.

She asked me to send her the photo, and she posted it all over social media, the modern equivalent of people in the Bible running to the city, saying: "Come and see. There is light." Gwen's story serves as an example for me that none of us needs to leave our common work of justice because it's hard or we are mad. We keep working for justice. We keep practicing peace.

. . .

GIVEN THAT WE are bound to grace, I would like to offer five practical ways to embrace grace to live more freely. The first is to *trust your passion*. This gives us the energy to work to gain the knowledge, experience, and expertise needed to carry us through to the next phase. The old saying is "Follow your heart." This concept gets more complicated when we add that, when passion intersects with the world's need, our purpose is born. I think, *Keep it simple: trust your passion.*

My third son, after he came home from college during the pandemic, announced to the family that he was switching from a major in math to a major in art. I almost laughed in joy and wonder, as the family all congratulated him. In the midst of the global crisis, where the entire world has determined whose work is essential and whose is not (and they definitely didn't have artists on their list of essential workers), he found his way to art. He said the protests and the pandemic had stirred the artist within him, and I salute him for starting out in this world following his passion. That is brave and right.

I, as a math major, would advocate that math, too, is an artistic endeavor and is one of the most practical and divine majors young seekers of truth can declare. Math is a universal language that is present in all aspects of our lives. Whether we are engaged in cooking, economics, biology, building, driving, playing music—it's all math. These activities are built on ideas and symbols that span the globe with regal simplicity.

Take the idea of seven. It evokes luck, disaster, heaven, prime, and creation. One simple idea representing stories, axioms, and truth. Now, imagine an infinite number of those symbols and how they open a new understanding of creation and possibility. Imagine that a sunflower is the perfect spiral or how tides affect the phases of our bodies. Rethink your affinity to math to translate the practical and divine nature of the universe. Before you say, "I'm no good at math," look at a circular clock with hour and minute hands. In that simple clock, a patient and kind teacher, so much of the universe can unfold. In the clock, you can find the world of trigonometry in the angles of the hands turning. You can then unfold the work of the spinning hands across an axis and see it wave. If you can begin to imagine the clock and the waves it produces, a world of possibilities and order opens up. When people say, "I have no idea how a radio works," you can imagine the clock and the sound wave over time, and begin to piece the mysteries of the universe together.

But I digress.

The second practical way to embrace our tie to grace is to *trust work more than inspiration.* Inspiration can be fickle. Just because we are passionate about something doesn't mean we'll be inspired every day. If we do the work, we can trust that inspiration will come. In the work of practically divine, the daily work is nine-tenths of love.

I have more than a few examples of the truth of this. One of the most concrete examples I have is building the café at Thistle Farms. It took longer and cost more than I thought it would. I was passionate about tea and serving it to people to build community, but once we got started, I knew I wasn't inspired to lay floors and paint walls and pick menus and pass inspections. Thank God for community and that we kept one another going through the whole thing. If I had waited to feel inspired, that building would still be boarded up.

The next step in remembering our bond to grace is to *form rituals.* I can't say this enough to you or to me: *To do the work of following your passions through the times you are uninspired, you need to have good rituals.* If you create rituals in the easier times, they will carry you through the harder ones.

My most basic daily rituals include brewing and stirring tea before the sunrise, walking and daydreaming at least one poetic line, and anointing myself before bedtime, with essential oils blended with moringa. My rituals around writing start with said tea in a bathtub, with some oils. I may not feel like writing, but I know if I can carry my cup of tea and sit in a steamy tub with geranium and lavender calling me to think, I will write. As I hear the water rushing to fill the tub, I can feel my writing self emerge.

When you carry on a ritual overtime, the ritual begins to comfort and call you. Practice the ritual to help the work flow.

For more than five years, when I go into Thistle Farms to get some work done, I have entered the campus through the café, and I get a cup of hot water with lemon. It is the only place I drink hot water and lemon, and I drink it there every time. Many rituals like this one are born in practicality. For instance, I didn't want anything that I'd need to ring up on the register, but wanted it to kinda feel like tea. This drink emerged and has kept me grounded while, on some days, the vortex of chaos spins. I sip my tea and walk through the spaces, greeting people and checking in on folks to see how they are faring

The next step in embracing grace is to *lead with love.* Sometimes we feel like we have to leave love at the door if we want to be successful, seem strong, and sound businesslike. Forget that. That is neither practical nor divine. Love is powerful, and once you are following your passions, it is love that will lead you. No matter what. Many successful businesses are born out of missions. The most successful ones never leave the mission behind. Love can be a powerful business model, it can form strategic plans, it can topple old babble like towers, it can dismantle oppression, it can be the bandleader of the protest, it can be the blueprint for new structures.

Several times over the years, special groups have come in to lead us in the latest ways to think strategically, work effectively, interact safely, and develop thoughtfully. The groups are helpful, with fresh eyes and new perspective. But over the years I have found, even as the language has changed and the marketing has been redone, a common thread is that they don't feel comfortable speaking about love as a strategic or core value.

Many times it feels like the strategic marketing groups are describing love, and sometimes it feels like they're creating a space for love, but they never say it. We can all think of reasons a strategic planning company—a.k.a. a brand-building company, a.k.a. a corporate leadership development team, and so on—doesn't feel comfortable saying to grown-ass people, "Our best advice is to 'lead with love.'" People will think you're next going to ask them to join hands and sing "Blowin' in the Wind." That is not what leading with love looks like. It looks like taking the highest attribute we assign to our creator and saying that we will follow this lead. We will measure all the other outcomes we have on the scale of love.

The last step on my top-five list of practical ways to embrace grace is *follow up*. Following up and cleaning up compose the difference between making a splash and planting good seeds that will bear great fruit. I wish I could tell you how long it has taken me to learn that putting things I need to do in a drawer is not taking care of them. I have grieved letters unanswered that seem impossible to resurrect now. I have hidden in shame from people

I didn't follow up with years ago. I am sure that everyone, as the sun sets and rises again, can feel the "oh, no" of things we left undone another day.

Follow up and clean up, tasks regulated to assistants and committees, are at the heart of our bondedness. This is where it comes full circle, and where we can tie the knot and begin again. Please don't miss out on this by leaving the painting tape on the corners of the room you painted and assume your mom will finish it up. When I called my son out on that recently, he said, while he was still playing a very attention-demanding gaming thing, that he wanted to make sure it was dry and that the color looked good in daylight.

"Honey, it's been three days," I reminded him.

"You can take the tape off," he said, "if it's bothering you."

I don't need to go into details, but he decided to get up and take the tape off.

* * *

SO, WE FOLLOW our passions, trust the work, form rituals, lead with love, and follow up. Simple as that. Until it isn't. Until we realize that being bound to grace doesn't stop the pain in this world and in our hearts. Sometimes we want the work to be pretty instead of deeply beautiful and painful. Sometimes we just want to feel the binds to grace; we don't want to be reminded of that attachment by going through hell. We want it to feel easy instead of intricate and deep. We want to think at some point that it's done, we have arrived, but the destination is still down the road.

While we're working to know freedom and justice because we are tied to grace, we retreat to places where we remember that binding. *Retreat* is more than a word called for in battle. It is a word called for when we desire renewal and remembrance. In the midst of my busiest seasons, I have to take to the woods. When tempers flare in the summer heat in our community and violence is a real threat, we all head out to the woods or on retreats to gain some perspective. This work of living into grace isn't easy or pretty, and it isn't done until they sprinkle dirt over us.

Lately, I have found myself retreating to the woods earlier and earlier, as the summer takes hold. The grace I have found on those mini retreats has saved me this year. This year, as the temperatures huddled in the nineties by mid-morning, we got our first snow from cottonwood trees. The flurry came in airy puffs, as fanciful as monarch wings dancing with dappled halos on a whimsical descent. Cottonwood snow lowers stress. When a puff lands on you, you should make a wish.

When this old world starts to get you down, I believe the best retreat is to turn to the essential woods, which invite us to remember our ideals and confess freely. It is to the woods that lovers of justice retreat every now and again, to stir their hearts and mind in the knowledge of love for all creation. The civil rights movement's grandfather, the Reverend Dr. Howard Thurman, retreated to the woods as a young child in Florida during the Jim Crow era, to find a space of freedom. He credits his relationship with an old oak tree with grounding him in his essential beliefs, including radical nonviolence, a concept that influenced young preachers like the Reverend Dr. Martin Luther King Jr.

This year, deep in the woods, I spoke among the cottonwood snow to a new leader, in his early twenties, of the Black Lives Matter movement in Nashville. He was talking quietly about his dream, which he said was a gift because so much of his time is spent using his loud voice to be heard through masks, smoke bombs, and tear gas. But I also think he was feeling the tenderness in the cottonwoods, to combat the stress and fear that come with bearing the yoke of leadership. We walked—no, strolled— for three hours. In the last hour, along with the cottonwood snow, a sweet rain washed our weary hearts.

Cottonwoods were here before brothers and sisters were dragged ashore and enslaved. They were here before settlers killed for what was not theirs. They witnessed lynchings, Freedom Rides, and secret longings. They silently bore decades in the alleys of Nashville, where we raped, addicted, and arrested our sisters. For the thirty years I have been a pastor in a small A-frame under cottonwood trees that snow every year around June. It was under those snowy trees that I dreamed of sanctuary for women in Nashville. This year, as the cottonwood snow falls again, it feels like a cleansing, reminding us we are traveling a long road, and we need strength to keep ourselves bound to one another.

After my friend left the woods, I took one more tiny stroll and lifted my head, squinting to see the source of the snow, and I saw a child's moon in the afternoon sunlight. I knew it would be another year before I could be washed in the cottonwood, and I wanted to glimpse the grace of the heavens falling in summer snow.

People have been working for justice since people began killing for power and intimidating by force. I imagine cottonwood snow tufts falling between the heavens and earth, holding the names of men and women who have lived for the sake of love in the work of justice. If we follow the steps that remind us of grace, and we keep heading to the woods, we will never lose that bond.

* * *

WHEN WE ARE bound to grace, it feels like there is more synchronicity in the events unfolding before us, instead of chance. I want to close out this chapter with a couple stories that remind us we are not spinning out—we are tied to grace. Both stories contain the hard reality of our humanity, but I hope both help you remember that even on the days you feel lost, grace has already found you.

The first story takes place as Nicholas Hitimana and I were standing in a beautiful geranium field in Rwanda. We had met in 2008, when I was looking for justice-oriented partners for Thistle Farms, to grow essential oils. Our paths seemed like they'd just happened to cross, since I was out there visiting another group. We met and became friends, and over the course of the next decade, we continued to support each other's work, learn from one another, and grow our justice enterprises.

His heroic story of surviving the genocide and escaping with his family to Scotland deserves its own book. His heroic story of returning to Rwanda to work with the widow survivors of the genocide could fill the second volume. There is much to admire about Nicholas, including his modesty and his ability to name injustices and then dream of solutions.

We both had made three or four trips to support each other as our enterprises were growing. On this trip, we had three main goals: develop a new oil blend together, start a rabbit fertilization project, and talk about cowriting an article about the value of the producer in the market chain. We were walking through a fragrant field when he stopped and turned toward me.

He asked, "What are the chances that we found each other all those years ago, and we would be wandering in the fields of Rwanda together still dreaming of the next steps?"

I told him I thought the chances were about 100 percent. It was inevitable, or as my mom would have said, "It was bound to happen, since we are bound to grace."

Both of us were broken and searching; both of us were drawn to the gift of healing oils. Of course we would find each other on the search. *Synchronicity*, that poor word overused in the late seventies, is still a great word to explain those moments of signs of grace—they are not random.

* * *

THE SECOND STORY is harder to tell but reminds me most about how my mom lived and died in a graceful state.

The most out-of-the-blue disease you probably could contract is Creutzfeldt-Jakob, a variant of "mad cow" disease, which attacks the brain. About twenty-five years ago, my mother was admitted to the hospital for an undiagnosed terminal illness, which we later found out was Creutzfeldt-Jakob. She was admitted to the hospital after we called an ambulance on the morning that she could no longer walk and was sitting in a wet mess in her bed.

I was about eight to ten weeks pregnant at the time and had woken up that morning bleeding. I was already a mess when my brother called, and I headed over to Mom's.

I saw her sitting in the bed with a kind of scary-calm expression, and she said: "I bet you think I am scared. I'm not."

Dear Lord, Mom, you should be, I thought. *I know I am scared as hell.*

I asked my brother to call an ambulance, and I called my doctor. I told my brother and sister I'd meet them at the hospital, but I was heading to my doctor first. After my doctor confirmed I was having a miscarriage, she said I either could be admitted or wait for the miscarriage to finish over the next few days. I felt lost and sad. As someone who thrives on as little medical intervention as possible, I decided to opt to let the miscarriage happen on its own time, and I drove to the hospital. On the way, I remember feeling like I wasn't sure what to pray for or to whom to turn.

My mom was settling in to her room when a nurse walked in and asked me if my mom was the wife of her childhood pastor. Since my father had only been the pastor for a year before the car crash, and that had been more than thirty years ago, it was shocking that she knew him and asked about him. I didn't think anyone in Nashville remembered him.

The nurse told me that my dad had been to her parents' house on a pastoral emergency, and it was when he'd left their house that the drunk driver killed him, less than a mile away and a few minutes after leaving the house. She said his sacrifice was what had saved her parents' marriage. I had never heard any part of that story.

"I am honored to take care of your mom," she said.

Was it inevitable that my mom contracted one of the deadliest prions on the planet? Or that I would miscarry on the same morning I learned that my mom was dying? Or that the one nurse in all Nashville who felt like she owed a piece of her life to my mom would walk in to care for her? I honestly don't know. What I do know is that even on the hardest days, if we can find the presence of mind to feel love's presence, a peace that passes understanding washes over us. We are not lost. In the practically divine, we experience the sweet feeling that, no matter where we are or how intensely we are feeling joy or grief, we are found.

• • •

AS WE END this sweet part of the book, where I got to remember my mom's passing and her gift of being bound to grace, all the time I still feel the wonder of how love searches for us and knows us. I remember reading in the book of Acts that we are groping for God, and God is never far away. That is the very essence of grace. To be bound by grace means that we are known by the source of all love. But it also means we are *willing to be hurt*. To be known, we have to share our intimacies and vulnerabilities. I am willing for my Creator, who knows and loves me, to see my vulnerability and weaknesses. If we hold that stuff in, it is hard to be known.

It is amazing to feel as though I can be in a safe enough space to trust those parts of me. I think it is part of why the Thistle Farms community has been around and growing for so long, because we try to say, "This is a safe space to be known, to expose your vulnerability." We try to say, "Be willing to trust love enough to discover that within our vulnerability is great strength."

To be known also means we are *brave enough to search our own hearts*. We have to be willing to continue to search our hearts. To be known means I will continue to look inward and say, "This is where I need to grow, this is the muse that is speaking to me, this is where I am being led, this is where I am broken."

Finally, to be bound by grace and to be known mean we are *willing to live with longing our whole life*. Does anyone think communion, where we receive a sip of wine and a taste of bread, sates our hunger? It is the longing to be known that propels us back into the world, to seek truth and justice. It is that propelling that allows us to be intimate with our community, our partners, our family, our friends. This longing is the poet's muse. When we live on the fringe of the fabric, we can see the beautiful pattern. It's not a curse. It's a gift. It is a gift to feel longing. Unrequited love keeps our desire for love strong. It is in our experience of searching that we become assured that God is searching, too.

It is easy to say no one knows me; it is harder to proclaim *I am known*. I have been bound by grace, and God knows me.

COME TO THE WOODS

Essential in pandemics, the woods call,

Come to us, unmasked and alone.

You who are weary of breathing your own stale words,

Come into our silence that transforms gasps into spirit.

Come close and walk softly on our hallowed ground,

Rediscovering the holiness of dirt.

Walk where the honeysuckle incense whispers joy

And choir birds sing to quiet your internal ranting.

Come dwell here when the congregations shutter,

And all the world shelters in but carries on.

Find your way into sweet shade where

The old legacy oaks telling their tales

Can once again be your refuge.

Come weep beneath the hickory leaves

Shimmering in a canopy when troubles press in.

They will keep you looking to the heavens

And dreaming of sweeter times.

Come cease your cell service among sassafras baby sprouts

To receive a reprieve from daily counts of disease.

Feel the paw paws petition you to utter words like

optimistic and *joy* without seeming ridiculous.

Come lie beneath a tulip poplar mast,

With billowed flowered bells that carry daydreams.

Wander in the gift of whim and fantasy

That awaken the spirit of peace.

Come smell cedar's aromatic memory

Filling you with delight beyond your intellect.

Sweet as ironweed dancing with walnut trees

Just because the wind blows.

Come fall on your knees when you cannot contain

The beauty of bluebells blooming near a spotted fawn

And give thanks for the essential woods

That have healed us again.

SIX

Holy Imperfect

I WAS AT A wedding reception when the mother of the bride whispered about one of the female guests: "That's just mutton dressed as lamb." That saying is both brilliant and mean. Condescending sayings like that one, even spoken in jest, are why millions of people dye their hair the same color as their friends, and why, in unison, the world raises and lowers hems based on what others deem right.

God forbid we are muttons dressed as lambs. God forbid we aren't perfectly quaffed or that our individual tastes stand out. I sometimes worry that my hair is too long for my age, or my dancing will lead people to think that *I think* I'm younger than everyone knows I am. I don't want them to be muttering that I'm mutton dressed as lamb.

Wouldn't the world be more fun if we were all free to dress like our own sheep selves as we deem beautiful? I still love my overalls from college and want to wear them whenever I damn well please, without judgment. I say let muttons dress as lambs all they like. We have a God-given right to celebrate ourselves and our imperfections as stamps of uniqueness. We are made in the image of love. But sometimes, when we're just ourselves, it's too much or not enough for people around us. However, I feel that imperfectly perfect is the way to live. Get to know yourself and celebrate the unique imperfections.

• • •

ABOUT A DECADE ago, I visited the house of a man of some prestige and power in Nashville. I was there to ask him about donating to a well project in Ecuador, to get water to the children in the school I had founded in my mother's memory. I thought we were having a good conversation, when he suddenly jumped on me as I sat on his couch. I pushed him off as he was trying to sexually assault me, and he simultaneously tried to humiliate me. He said he wasn't clear on what the parameters were around our relationship, because I spoke and dressed so casually. He went on to say that I invited his kind of behavior because I was too "open."

I was in my forties at the time, way over trying to nego-
tiate these troubled waters from men in power, and the
man in this story was in his late sixties. I had been ordained for fifteen years, was married, and had three children. *In my openness, maybe I am mutton trying to act like
lamb*, was the basic message of shame rising in my spirit.
I hate that he thought I was flirting. Was I? was one of the
thousands of thoughts that crept through my head over
the next few days. I'm imperfect, but I definitely didn't invite him to jump on me, and I'm cognizant enough about
myself to clarify parameters, for anyone who wants to ask.
Thankfully, I had built enough stable boundaries to not let
him live inside my head long. *He was gross*, I reminded
myself over the next couple days. *I am fine.* I am imperfectly perfect in my skin and in my heart. I don't want to
live not being open, or I might become someone I don't
recognize.

That's my hope for everyone reading this—that above
both the noisy and silent criticism, you feel your imperfectly perfect self dancing for the sake of the dance that
feeds your soul, and not because it is a dance expected of
you. Whatever the saying is about muttons and lambs in
whatever part of the world you're from, those sayings are
created solely to remind us that we're imperfect, and
everyone knows it. The antidote for experiencing "chronic
imperfection worry" isn't striving harder for perfection—
it's finding the *practically divine in the imperfection.*

• • •

THE NOTION THAT something can be perfectly imperfect or creatively imperfect, and thus unique, is what
compels artists and writers. It is at the soul of their work.
As we're closing the chapter of our world pandemic, I have
watched all the artists in my family up close for months,
and they have fed my belief in the truth of the *imperfect
perfect*. All four men who live with me, my husband and
three sons, are artists. I have watched them paint, create
video content, host cowriting sessions on the platform
Zoom, and draft on their Microsoft Surfaces. It is a win-
dow into the world of holy and creatively imperfect. I
sometimes listen in as the speakers echo the "Zoom
writes" throughout the house, and I can hear writers from
Ireland, Nashville, and New York are dialed in to my living
room. I can hear the individual accents chiming in with
ideas born in their hearts, to put out into the world. Their
sayings and melodies rise not in fear, but in wonder.

I heard my husband talk about why live drums are better, precisely because they're not perfect. "There is life
when there are rough edges," he said.

When I see my son imagine a ten-foot mural with a
Madonna rising from the waves, I want to shout,
"Hallelujah—you are amazing!" Slowly, he paints what has
lived in his head and brings it to life. When I try on a prototype of my eldest son's new T-shirt line, which bears the
logo he made sitting poolside in quarantine, I marvel at
where beauty comes from and how it is stamped by one's

own vision. When my youngest son hands me his laptop Surface, to reveal the superhero he has created, flying on a rocket holding sparklers, I laugh with wonder and joy.

It all inspires me, and, collectively, they make me want to lean into my imperfections and notions of beauty more and more. It makes me grateful that I am still open and still have a thought that rises from my own imperfect heart. None of the artists I live with are interested in perfection; they are interested in the truth of the beauty in creation. It must be how our creator feels at our efforts to express the practically divine truth in our thoughts, words, and deeds.

My oldest son first attended art school in St. Petersburg, Florida, to explore writing and painting. After I dropped him off, I spent the night nearby and then visited the Dalí Museum (as in Salvador Dalí) the next day, to kill some time before later meeting up with my son for our last supper. I was kind of in a daze and just wandered in, simply surprised that this famous Spanish artist even had a museum in Florida. As I learned the story of how he got there and the trials and success of his journey into art, I fell in love. Salvador Dalí's explaining how he came to accept the imperfections within his body of work drew me deeper in.

Learning about artists' unique imperfections do not call us to disillusionment; they call us to a revived humanity. It was incredible to view a portfolio of seeming perfection on display in huge works. But this artist, celebrated for his technical skill and precise draftsmanship, was quoted as saying, "Have no fear of perfection—you'll never reach it." If he could live with the art created by perfect imperfection at its best, we all can.

I can imagine him getting up early to wax his incredible, thin, long mustache, getting as close to perfection as possible in his appearance before his brush ever hit a canvas. To know he believed perfection to be an impossible goal and to let it go is the stuff revivals are made from. I am free! Yes! I feel my soul singing in his declaration. I am perfectly and holily imperfect. Hallelujah. Beauty and ingenuity live in the heart of practically divine, while perfection dwells in desert mirages and fantasy.

Dalí confirmed what I'd known my whole life to be true: handmade may not be perfect, but it is perfectly imperfect. Throughout this manuscript, I have tried to celebrate everything handmade and divine. I have celebrated women I know who have created something beautiful from the pieces of their lives. I believe their work should be lauded around the world as radical, economical, moral, and spiritual. I learned this by osmosis from my mother, who cherished all the art any child ever made for her. She loved painted macaroni necklaces we made so much that they were still tucked away inside her dresser when she died. She loved them; she wasn't just being nice. She could see their beauty and value. She had those kinds of eyes. If we made something, it was beautiful because we made it. For her, our childhood fingers changed the essence of the materials, transforming them into something bigger. When I first learned to crochet, I made a chain about a hundred feet long and transformed the ceiling light, in the middle of the bedroom my sister and I shared, into a chandelier. I took the single long chain and taped it, then let a big loop hang and taped it again, repeating the process all around the light. Then I went around the whole light again, repeating the pattern with smaller loops, so there were layers to the loops, and I thought it looked like a fancy chandelier you might see in a mansion. I cut out a few pieces of aluminum foil and made small balls and attached them to the bottom of each loop, like crystal prisms. My sister laughed at my effort, but my mom couldn't believe it. She was delighted, and I kept it up for almost a week, until the tape gave out.

The finest example I can give that highlights the truly imperfect perfection in creating something from our hands and hearts, I learned from deep in the hills of Chile. That country suffered greatly under a fearful and deadly regime in the early 1970s. One of the most beloved women of Chile, and the bestselling Latinx author alive, is Isabel Allende, who had to flee her home country during that time. I am honored to count Isabel as a friend and a donor who helped Thistle Farms establish a global marketplace to celebrate women artisans around the world. For more than a decade now, her foundation, run by Lori Barra, has sustained the effort to support true craftmanship as revolutionary and healing. The sewers from Chile are amazing teachers who have taken the idea of cultivating beauty from the brokenness to an imperfect perfection.

A museum described the women of Chile who were quilting squares as having hands like wings of little birds—meaning that they were moving swiftly to stay afloat. We can conjure up the image easily enough for ourselves. Women in pueblos, living outside the big city of Santiago for years, knew one another and had always shared their individual burdens, griefs, and fears. Poverty was a common theme, so in the afternoons it was necessary to gather and get creative in how they could care for their families and community. In 1973, they still came together to sit with a few of their friends on church grounds, even as people were "disappeared" by the government, and violence was a real threat to all their families. Together they figured out how to get groceries, plant vegetables, make it through another day, and maybe share the heavy yoke they each were bearing.

But as with women around the world, even in crisis, you can't just sit around—you have to be busy doing something. So, with the help of the church, as they gathered and talked, they took out their needles, threads, and scraps of cloth. Maybe some of the cloth was from pieces of clothing from the man or child who'd gone missing during the latest round of violence by the Pinochet regime. Gradually, over the course of their common yet deeply personal struggles, with each thread they began to claim their humanity and lives back in the wondrous protest that is art at its finest. Like the thousands of pieces sewn together, they told a global story about the suffering of the poor at the hands of the powerful. They wove the truth that, together, in the face of that suffering, we still hope and we still love. Each hand-stitched square told a powerful, individual, and collective story. Some asked where the disappeared people had gone; some showed the violence in planes, police, and burning; and some showed grieving women gathered in protest. What is so remarkable about this protest through quilting and the artisan survivors who made the pieces is that the crafted squares aren't heartbreaking as much as heart strengthening. When I look at these creations, I feel that if these women could stitch them while they were living through that, we can figure out how to live creatively, peacefully, powerfully, and lovingly. All we need is a few scraps and maybe a couple friends.

*   *   *

WHETHER I'M ADMIRING my son's creations, Dalí's vision, or the craftsmanship of the Chilean women, I can see with my mother's eyes the truly beautiful gifts of our imperfect efforts. I am convinced beyond measure that a lack of perfection is no reason not to experience the divine. In fact, those small, imperfect perfections lead us to the foot of the divine.

One of the great prophets of the twentieth century explained that she didn't want people to call her a saint. She wasn't even trying for perfection. She was human, like all of us seeking spaces, like small cracks where justice can seep in with a bit of grace. Sermons and poetry and songs all remind us that the cracks are where the light shines in. We know that light shining through the cracks and ordinary people, not saints, do the heavy lifting. We know these truths for everyone—*but sometimes not for ourselves*. Our cracks are not where most of us feel light beams shining down. Most of us patch up our cracks with duct tape or whatever we can get our hands on, so no one can see. It's easy enough to see beauty in the imperfection of others, but it is another thing to see it in ourselves.

When I go on a rant and lose my vision of the beauty of imperfection, the brief internal conversation of chaos goes something like this:

> Everyone but me is perfectly imperfect. I am a mess. I am mutton dressed as lamb. I should be ashamed, but I still want you to feel wonderful. Stop it. I am being ridiculous. I am okay in my skin. As long as I don't stare too long in mirrors and keep looking at my hands, I am good.

"All is well, all is well, and all shall be well," whispers Julian of Norwich, from a thousand years ago, into my ear, and I always believe her. I have gotten the rant down to just a couple seconds . . . not bad. Then, once again, I can let go of the ideal of perfection and experience beauty.

Once, I was in a parking lot when I was going through this self-scolding at my imperfections. I was about to give a speech at a college, and I couldn't find my notes anywhere. I searched the car thoroughly. I had worked on the speech and was ready to wow them with some poetic metaphors and dazzling insights. I got out of the car, grieving my stupidity at losing the speech, walked into the auditorium, and spoke off the cuff. Of course, I wandered a bit into the weeds.

After the speech, I was telling myself that my speaking career was probably over, that my friends would leave me, and the work of justice enterprise I had dedicated my life to would shutter. Right then, a student came up to me and told me it was as if I had written that speech just for her, that she had been carrying the secret of her abuse, and now she was ready to tell someone and start healing. As she hugged me, I heard a strange sound. It was my speech. While we were driving to the college, I'd stuck the two pages of notes in my bra. It had been there all along. That close-to-perfect speech was tucked away.

The speech I'd given wasn't close to perfect, but it was exactly right. It was what was needed for that coed that day. I love it when things sometimes are simply perfect, not in their execution, but in their grace.

When we can let go of the perfect ideal, there is real life and joy on the other side. Holidays that never live up to the hype can be enjoyed. We can accept that, as parents, there are no ideal vacations, just parenting in different locations. Relationships, unfolding in reality before us, can be infused with humor and longevity. It's hard not to idealize situations, though. I remember when my three boys were between the ages of four to ten, and I was preparing to open the tea shop at Thistle Farms. My husband and I took an odyssey with our sons to Seattle, Washington, so I could learn more about tea. I signed us all up for a Japanese tea ceremony, believing I could learn about the art of hosting a tea ceremony and give my sons the gift of peace and tranquility. I had read about the way of tea and studied the ceremonies in books. I had helped launch a new tea company in Uganda and was close to opening the café serving tea in Nashville, so I wanted to experience a tea ceremony for myself and my family. I wanted to understand why three major philosophies (Confucianism, Taoism, and Buddhism) used tea, the oldest cultivated beverage in the world. So, I made my way to a real Japanese tea ceremony, led by a tea master in Seattle. When I imagined the ceremony, somehow, I was wearing a beautiful kimono and my kids had on slippers.

It felt like a shock to me that my boys didn't want to sit through an hour-and-a-half ceremony in a hot, sticky hut outside a garden as we crouched on our knees. Somehow, when I was researching, I'd missed the part saying it takes about forty-five minutes before you even take the first sip of tea. A tip I would give moms bringing children to the ceremony is to give them tea and snacks before you arrive. Do not, under any circumstances, arrive early. Also, if it's hard to understand the person giving the ceremony demonstration, this increases the fidgeting about 100 percent. The reality of sitting on my knees also made me want to ask them why they didn't sell kneepads right outside the hut. It would be a moneymaker for them and cut down on the pain I was feeling in my right knee about ten minutes into the ceremony.

All I am saying is that the reality of the tea ceremony was quite different from the tea party I'd conjured in my head. I didn't grasp the reality of what it would be like for forty-five minutes, to turn our teacups and listen. It was less dreamy and romantic than in my imagination—and it was better.

The heat and pain made what was unfolding before us more precious. I realized it was a discipline, and the people performing the ceremony were masters. The heat and pain added to the wonder that this was their life, before we were halfway through. Right before us, with smells of tea brewing and sounds of thick Japanese sandals walking across the wooden floor, we witnessed the most beautiful and intricate arm gestures for moving tea into the pot. The reality, not the dream, is what was life-changing for me and helped me dedicate the next five years to the study of justice and tea and to launch new tea companies and open a café.

I spent the ceremony trying to feel at peace as best as I could, while at the same time casting a few sideways glares at my kids, to communicate to them to sit still and not touch anything. Finally, when the host poured a tiny bit of tea into our tiny cups, the bitter green froth didn't taste that good. None of my kids drank it. They just waited patiently while we continued the ceremony. That was the most amazing part. I didn't like the taste of it, and it didn't matter. I could appreciate it. I could admire the time and talent and treasure it took. I could appreciate the palate I would need to develop in order to appreciate this new way. We had lived through an entire ceremony, and all my sons bowed at the end. It threw me, in a good way, to realize that all of us could be in a position to learn something new. I learned about intention, about ritual, about humility. I am so glad I got to sit through it.

Experiencing life, instead of living with the idea that some ideal thing is waiting out there, is how you live practically divine in the midst of imperfectly perfect. You don't have to wait to see beauty in a perfectly set diamond. If your ideal of beauty lies within the rarest gem, you'll miss the glory of the commonplace quartz on the trail that sparkles like a star in sunlight. If you wait for the impossible perfection of the ideal of justice, you'll never be able to jump into the fray and help make a difference. If I'd waited for the ideal scenario to unfold to do this work, I'd still be sitting in a library poring over all the wisdom I needed to seek. We can do the work practically and with divine inspiration, even as we seek the wisdom.

People have discarded their beauty and indwelling potential because of the imperfections woven into our DNA. If we don't discard those parts of ourselves that shine in imperfection, and instead distill them for the truths they reveal, we will find extraordinary brilliance. When we celebrate the practical perfection of a quartz, we want to search anew all the places within and behind us where we might have missed some gems. The places and stories that have carried us to this place of practically divine sometimes have been scary and lonely, but they can still hold truth and beauty to get us where we need to travel.

We can even begin to regain our humor, when we allow the impossible bar of perfect to be taken down a notch. As my son was getting ready to head back to school last fall, without realizing it, I found myself doing things my mom would do. One morning, around six o'clock, I was using a carpet shampooer to clean up all the nasty dog hair and young man dirt from the entire upstairs. When the carpet cleaner bumped into his door, where he was still asleep, I started laughing.

Oh, my Lord, I am my mother. This is exactly what she would do. Start cleaning way too early and wake someone up by accidently bumping the vacuum into the door.

I pretend I am not as imperfect as my mom, because I use all-natural products and don't douse my vegetables in cream of mushroom soup, but, oh, Lord, I am. I am as irritating and anxious for stuff to get done. I can make an itinerary for a vacation and then get my feelings hurt when my ne'er-do-well kids just want to lie around. There is nothing like laughing at our own holy imperfections. Comics, theologians, and writers fare much better when they can.

* * *

WHEN I BEGAN working with women coming off the streets and out of prison, I quickly learned I was meeting myself. I felt like I had more in common with the women coming through the doors than with most of my fellow priests. These women and I had similar imperfect qualities that I found endearing and beautiful. I was free to laugh and share with them in a way I couldn't with any other group of friends. Together, we found humor in the creepy men of our past, the things our moms did when there was no money, or how easily we are triggered. Early on, I knew I was doing the work *alongside* survivors, not *for* survivors. I knew, from the first time I shared a cigarette behind one of our smoke-free residential homes, that I was sitting with sisters. We were women who had what some call "thick skin" and could laugh stuff off that made other people feel a bit more fragile. But, after time passes and trust grows, and that thick skin smooths out, there was a tenderness that feels others' pain with an acuteness born out of pain on a cellular level. When I think of holy imperfect perfection, a hundred women survivors pop up like a carousel of heroic images.

Right at the top of that scrolling list of imperfect stunningness is Penny. Her raspy voice from Alabama echoed the injustices and humiliations I have heard in the universal language of childhood trauma. But she could tell that universal story with humor and power that would leave you laughing and crying.

One time, we were traveling together to speak at a university and crossed the Alabama border toward her home. She said something about knowing people would recognize her because, for a season, she was on the opener of the TV show *Cops*.

"What?" was all I could think to ask.

What unfolded next was a story of an unbelievable survival instinct, including the funniest description of trying to fit under a cheap hotel bed in Alabama when she saw the police coming. The clip from the show reveals two cops dragging her out from under that bed with all their might, while the song "Bad Boys" plays in the background.

I begged her to tell the rest of story and explain why in God's name she would let them put that on the air. She told me she let them use the clip for the show, because if she signed the paper, they'd let her walk, and all she wanted to do was leave the hotel room and go get high.

The story of what happened to Penny is too graphic and horrible to write on these pages. I hope that story turned to ashes, along with her body that passed too soon from the struggles of addiction and abuse. And I hope she always knew that all of us who loved her knew she was a victim way before they named her a criminal.

If you had asked Penny what her imperfection was, she might say something similar to what she told NPR in the early 2000s, when she was interviewed as one of the great survivor heroes. She told the interviewer that people thought she was tough because she was a survivor living under a bridge for seven years, using a CB radio to find truckers. But, she said, "I am really just a softy that cries all the time." In a voice laced with decades of smoke, she described how, since she was a little girl sitting at the beer joint with her dad, she'd cry if anything was hurt. She reminisced about how she used to cry at night because she was scared she would be raped before the morning. She said she cried for others hurt, because she knew how hard it was. On the way home from Alabama, at a Cracker Barrel store in Huntsville, she bought a package of butterfly magnets to give to her girlfriend. She was a softy, and I believe that was her superhero power.

When we recognize that our connection with one another is bound by our imperfections, rainbows and butterflies appear in front of gray clouds. We think we need to play it close to the vest, when sometimes we need to take the vest off.

This fall, Hall Cato, Thistle Farms CEO and an amazing leader and advocate for women, has been talking to me about the struggles of leading. He said: "I wanted to tell a woman sitting at the picnic table outside by the manufacturing building, crying, that I feel as empty as she does, but nobody wants to hear that from the leader. COVID-19, loneliness, bad sleep habits, the awful way we treat one another in this country, and so on—it's all catching up with me." Hal is one of the more compassionate and loving people I have met. And I believe the woman he is talking about may have wanted to hear that more than anything. I told him I thought his sentiment was an echo of words of saints for centuries. He is proclaiming: "I am holy imperfect and feel exhausted and broken, but I still keep going. So can you." When the shiny vest of perfection is peeled off, talk is truth, and we all breathe deeper. It binds us to each other, knowing we need one another.

We are bound by our imperfections, which help us remember that what we hold in common is more powerful than the lines we have drawn to separate ourselves. We created distinctions to separate ourselves one from another to try to seem more perfect. We separate ourselves, one from another, into categories that disrupt community and relationships.

Penny Hall and all her survivor sisters make it clear that the line between criminal and victim is blurry. I've met thousands of women with criminal records who were categorically victims long before we criminalized them. We can hold compassion for everyone, including women sitting in prison for violent crimes, if we're willing to hear the story and see our imperfect selves in that story. Most of us are both broken and have broken others, to varying degrees, but we know both sides. When we admit it and forgive it, it is practically divine. That is how the radical nature of the practically divine works in us and through us. When we work out the practical aspect of divinity, it offers us a way to serve one another, knowing we are all related.

* * *

THIS IS SOME of the best news in the whole world, that our imperfections are where divine freedom lives. We receive the gifts of community and connection—and divine gifts—from our imperfections, our missing pieces, and even our trauma. There is no better philosophy in this world to explain this than *wabi-sabi*. *Wabi-sabi* is the Japanese concept of embracing the imperfect. Beyond a concept, though, it's a way of finding beauty in what is considered "flawed" or "incomplete." When we let go of the illusion of perfection, there is freedom and meaning we never expected. It is the same philosophy as seeing the beauty of stained glass made from broken pieces, or the wonder of delicious soup made from chicken bones and vegetable scraps to create a delicate broth. In the broken pieces we have gathered to craft our stained glass, we recognize a beautiful creation of our own making. In the places and times we are most vulnerable, we can find the most divine gifts.

When we accept the beautifully imperfect all around us, there is freedom to move gracefully from the past and into the future through the present. There are even freedom and gifts in some of the trauma we have known. I cannot speak to anyone else's experience, but trauma gave me a different way of seeing the world and a longing that nothing could fill. It's not a longing for something in particular. I just have a deep sense of longing that might best be described as unrequited love. But along with that deep longing, the trauma gave me resiliency, courage, and compassion. Because of what I went through, I can trust myself to persevere. I can read a room and trust my gut. Because I was broken open, I learned how to scour the world for clues and fellow pilgrims. I am brave; I am vulnerable; I am still searching for the missing pieces and answers to *why*, in woods, in community, in books, and in friends. So, I am still learning! I have spent most of my life in the weeds, searching for the beautiful missing pieces, and that is where I find the best lessons.

• • •

IF WE CAN'T be perfect or it can't be perfect or we can't devote our life to it, sometimes we decide not to try it at all. But an act of love doesn't have to be perfect to be divine. In our pursuit of living in the practically divine, it is helpful to surrender our idea of perfection. We don't have to be perfect to be useful or beautiful. In fact, what we're missing, what is imperfect about us, is what makes us able to keep looking for and experiencing the divine. If we can love the imperfect parts of ourselves, we can find the strengths those "flaws" have given us and see the divine purpose in what is missing.

ALMOST PERFECT BEACH DAYS

Walking on sand tunes ears to the sound

Of crushed shells underfoot.

Toiling the year for a week of respite

Barely gives a base for basking before the sun.

Oh, those almost perfect sweet days!

Standing at the edge of crashing waves,

As children jump in gleeful anticipation.

Racing hearts, steadying unstressed before the horizon

Remembering the roundness of our island home.

The sky's expanse inviting dreams while

Holding the sun and the moon together gracefully.

Oh, those almost perfect days!

Low-tide walks reveal all that has been hidden.

Uncovering sand dollar treasures and unspoken dreams.

Midnight high tides wash daily tracks and dreamy castles

Into their rightful place called yesterday.

The ocean says welcome home.

Oh, those almost perfect days!

When we die what is left is dirt and ashes

But for now we are filled with ocean tears and sweat.

Saltwaters reveal the truth that poetry begets poetry.

In foaming wakes our mind wanders far enough

To find its way back to our own heart.

I am young and I am old in waves.

Oh, those almost perfect days!

| SEVEN |

Three Moves

AMONG THE PHRASES MY mom left me, like an inheritance that increases in value with time, one of the richest is "three moves are as good as a fire." That phrase is like a beautiful old merlot left sitting on the back shelf of memory. In that cool and quiet space, a complex chemical reaction occurs over time, quenching the thirst for wisdom while navigating life experiences. It is similar to the reaction that occurs among sugars and phenolic compounds in a red wine—it becomes rich with tannins and aromas.

When it's finally fermented, and we are ready to blow off the dust and uncork the phrase, we crave the depth of taste and meaning it offers. Decanting and pouring out an old saying from that back shelf ignites new ideas, like the tingle in the back of our throats with only a sip. Old phrases rekindle our palate for truth, as they easily carry us over time and space. We can laugh and cry as rich memories circulate throughout our being. Sometimes, when I carefully select a phrase from the pantry of my mother's sayings, it is so much like selecting an old wine that I know it's going to take up the rest of my day. Seriously—hurricanes, fires, or a bomb detonation can be occurring right now in the world, but I can dive into one of her old sayings and be carried back thirty years in the blink of an eye. I pick the phrase up, turn it around a bit, think of her, and make a dreamy space to drink from her cup.

The phrase "three moves" applies to many situations. Feel free to use it whenever you like. None of my mom's phrases are copyrighted; they're out there for anyone's use, like the thousand other phrases from the mother-line we soaked up throughout our lives, like gravy on our biscuits. The "motherline" refers to the unbroken chain of wisdom or customs we learn from our mothers, which we often don't remember learning! It's just part of the collective wisdom passed down from mothers. In my mom's language, the phrase "three moves" means we can travel further and unencumbered if we let stuff go. The longer we keep dragging along literal and figurative stuff from our past, the sicker we become of it. By the time we have carried some of that stuff for three moves, we may, in fact, finally be able to leave it behind. Thus, three moves are as good as a fire. What I have come to understand about this, as I swirl the phrase around the cup like wine to see if it has legs ("legs" is a wine-tasting term that describes the droplets that form along the edge of the glass and indicate the quality of the wine you're about to taste), is that *carrying around less junk is living a practically divine way of life.*

The place I need to apply this phrase is to the baggage I carry around surrounding my first abuser. You may remember, at the beginning of this book, that old, creaky door that was opened again by my abuser's grandson when he came into the café. After my interactions with him, I was tormented, as I have been for decades, torn between feeling righteous, responsible, and reprehensible. I had a reprieve from all of it for almost a whole year until recently, when he popped back into my text feed.

What I have longed for my whole life was to wrap up those years of trauma in a beautiful box that I could set next to those sweet old sayings on a back shelf. They could easily travel with me, but they would be pretty and light. But that isn't how it works in the practically divine way. No matter what kind of box you put trauma in, you still have to carry it with you whenever you want to move.

It was a gift that when the episode with the grandson blew up, he had to go his own way as the pandemic shuttered the world. Now that I have let that past go, I'm not interested in packing it all back up and carrying it with me. It's done, and I know it's done, because there isn't any energy around it anymore. I am lighter because I have moved on without it. That feels as close to a miracle as I know, and I pray that in all the writing I have done, if you can let one thing go—I mean, really let something go—you will feel like this whole read was worth it.

I have learned, in the best practically divine way, that freedom lies in the metaphorical burning of something, so we can't keep it with us. We don't have to make it right for everyone. Burn the damn things you have been lugging around. I can burn my need for closure, I can burn my ephemeral longing to rewrite that broken chapter, I can burn my guilt that I wasn't a good pastor to the grandson. Offer it all as a sacrifice laid on the altar of my youth. Maybe watch the flames and dance at my unbridled heart, free of carrying it all around. Then walk on the holy ashes and rubble left behind, remembering the sacred in the remains.

Rubble offers a place to begin to rebuild from ashes. Even after horrible forest fires, in rich alkaline ash, new trees and fire weed start to grow. There are even some species of pines that cannot release their seeds until there is a fire. Walking through the rubble of a burned forest, along with the great loss, you can smell new sap and hear bird calls like promises. Old burned trunks and tiny twigs are already being used by animals looking for safe housing. Light hits the forest floor in wide beams unattainable when thick, leafy branches had kept it shaded. There is new life in the rubble; it just takes practically divine eyes to see it.

During the early hours of Christmas Day 2020 in Nashville, a bomb detonated on Second Avenue. You could hear it, like a big construction project or something, echo in the quiet morning after a pretty silent night. Almost all communication on the internet and telephone systems ceased because of the bombing. That afternoon, my husband and I drove around a completely closed downtown, to listen to the radio and glimpse the rubble.

Rubble is everywhere in our lives, like leftovers or jobs that have gone awry. Rubble is found after the breakup, in the aftermath of pandemics, and in the wasteland of generational injustices. However, this rubble from the bomb was fresh. It still carried smoky grief and shock. We could only see it while peering through an alleyway, but I knew that beneath it all, there would be a rebirth, if we could remember that our desire to love and create is so much stronger than a bomb.

That street was a nucleus of music life in Nashville. It housed concert venues, hostels, hotels, and businesses that cater to the millions of tourists who come to share the wonder of music. And in an instant, more than forty buildings were damaged or destroyed, and no carriage rides were going to carry people up the twinkling, lit street. In the rubble and remnants of those buildings, new dreams can be born.

I am dedicating the next chapter of my life to reflecting on the practically divine nature of remnants and rubble. I will knit with discarded pieces of yarn; I will write from old words re-stitched together and repurposed. I will let go of rotting things and ideas and build something new and useful. When we let go, something new comes.

The only way I know how to burn what I need to let go of and sift through the rubble to find new life is through the most practical tool we have in our lives—forgiveness. I wish there was another way, but after a half century of trying, it's the best I've got. Forgiveness is the work of the saints who proclaim it as a path to freedom. It liberates us when we don't want to be bound by what has been done to us or what we have done to ourselves. Mohandas Gandhi, the guru of liberation, said: "The weak can never forgive. Forgiveness is the attribute of the strong." And the beloved civil rights leader and teacher James Cone said forgiveness is "victory out of defeat. It is the weak overcoming the strong."

* * *

ALONG WITH FORGIVING, we concurrently get to cultivate the fine art of grieving. If we're burning and letting things go, we had better be ready to grieve. Walking through rubble is the best metaphor for grieving I know. Sifting through the broken bits and deciding which to scrap and which you can rebuild into a beautiful stained glass or repurposed art takes years. Grief is a brave and relentless teacher. Each new episode of grief offers new lessons, but new grief also connects us to all our old grief. The bravest way to live the three moves is to not shy away from mourning the passing of something beloved. Loneliness and melancholy, grief's byproducts, make us doubt whether we can make it through our grief. While it feels heavy to grieve, it is how we honor losing what we love.

A friend recently lost her child, and she told me she wanted the daughter's funeral to be "like she was still here." My heart was breaking for her. It is a hard row to hoe to live like your daughter, who is dead, is still alive because of the fear of grieving. We don't get to choose what we grieve. Our hearts will do that work for us. But grieving is the heavy lifting of loving. The only thing heavier is carrying the burden of not grieving. Carrying the weight of the ungrieved buckles us. That is enough to make us a shell of who we are, numb, bitter, and fragile. Life and love are precious, and it is good and right that we should be sad to let them go in grief.

I started grieving my mom's death as she lay dying. So many of my friends talk about the ongoing sweet grief of mothers who loved well. One of my friends, whose mother had died years before, said it best the other day: "I just want to talk to her and catch her up on the last five years."

When my mom was dying, I sat by her bed and tried to remember everything, but what I took away from the wake was that even the people I love the most never knew her fully. Even with those we are closest to, there are parts of them that may never fully be known. That is good and hard news. It means the people I am closest to might have burdens and secrets they carry that they have never forgiven or grieved. They may not have practiced three moves and will die with unnecessary burdens of shame and secrecy.

* * *

THE IDEA OF three moves offers us, known only fully to ourselves, a way to let go. Eventually, all those things will die with us. Our old, shameful secrets are like withered spiders on dusty cobwebs. Sweep them out, because there is no virtue in leaving them to take up space and gather more dust. Our secret truths don't have to make us strangers. We can still love and grieve and practice three moves.

As best as I can know a person, I knew and loved my mom. The grief I held for her was profound. I knew she would never know all my children, I knew that her work wasn't finished, and I knew I'd never again kiss the woman who gave me life, sustained me, and loved me.

Several months after her death, I found a hair from her long brown braid on my couch. She was sixty-two when she died and didn't have a gray hair on her head. She wore her hair in a single braid down her back. When I found that piece of hair, I cried all over again. That grief, long after the death grief, was the most private grief. I walked out my door and cast the hair into the tiny thicket of private bushes and kudzu next to our house and hoped a bird would use it for a nest. My mom was practical until the end.

• • •

SHE USED TO say, "Don't bury money." Do it on the cheap. She said we were dirt and angels, and both were useful. She had no patience for long services or funeral homes. She wanted us to love her deeply but not "wallow" in it. She wanted us to practice three moves. And she was right. I have seen "three moves" work like magic on people when I visit them in the hospital.

I remember one couple, who'd been married more than thirty years. The wife asked me to come see them in the hospital after her husband's long illness. She greeted me at the door and said she felt incredibly happy, not despite the cancer but in part because of the cancer. She said: "There is only enough space in this hospital room for me—I can't bring my old luggage and resentments with me. I finally let it all go. Now we are free to love each other, and it is amazing."

The same is true when I'm called to visit a family keeping vigil in a hospice. They are deep into their "three moves" and letting go of so much. I try not to pretend I know what their prayer is or what they need to let go of. Instead, I try to honor the grief present and the grief yet to come. It is a place to walk softly. Not too long ago, I was called to give last rites to a friend's mom. The room was hallowed as three people sat quietly around the bed. I set my phone and keys down, we held hands, and I offered a prayer and anointed her forehead with oil. Her three children wept, and I tiptoed out to leave them with their mom.

Poignant and good. About halfway down the hospice hall-way, I realized I'd left my phone and keys by the bedside. Opening the door and tiptoeing back in, my friend laughed, patiently holding my stuff in her hand. "I was waiting for you to come back," she said, laughing.

I swear, laughing by a deathbed is an unbelievably holy act. Humor is miraculous and brave. Humor in grief is grace. It is a way to help us let go even as we are clinging.

However, some things I can't let go of yet. Some things we want to hold on to and maybe carry for just one more move. When we cut off my mom's braid, I laid it in plastic inside my bedside table, so no one could see it. It was like a relic to me, of resilience and love. Kind of like a small piece of cloth from a saint, a relic from a battlefield, a piece of an old brick taken from the rubble. It wasn't something you took out to admire, like a prism in light. It was closer to something hidden that kept you safe.

About a year after her death, I took her braid out and rebraided it into a thin, twelve-foot-long, continuous cord. I don't know why, but as I've mentioned, I go to crafts when I get in a pinch. I painted a tree on a canvas and glued her cord of hair onto the outline of what was emerging as a family tree. It sounds gross writing it, but at the time, it worked for me.

I took some ashes from the Ash Wednesday service, blended it with holy oils, filled the tree in, and wrote the names of every person I have ever loved. Of course, over the last few decades, that strange piece of grieving art has moved a few times, and I have no idea where it is. Three moves end up winning in the end. Braiding her hair was a step in letting go and remembering that everything but love dies. Like fire, ashes to ashes.

The grief in three moves is the cleansing. I presided at the funeral of a young man who'd died suddenly in an accident. His family didn't know who to call, and they got my number. I had never met any of them, but at the funeral, I cried along with a thousand other people. Maybe because the violin played an old, familiar Irish melody, maybe because the cream-colored bulletin I was holding felt exactly like the paper of a hundred other funerals, maybe because diffused light in afternoon sun through stained glass melts hearts. And maybe because I am human, and grief is the cleansing of our hearts, so we can love. Maybe we all cry when we remember how close to dust we are and how everything but love dies. We need the gift of grief to help us let it go.

*   *   *

BESIDES DEATH, ANOTHER reason we hold on to so much junk is fear. When we're scared, we're failing and afraid to show it, so we get stuck. Our imagination closes down. When we don't think we'll be loved if we are truly known, to ourselves or others, we feel like we have to surround ourselves with comfort things, and that just about kills our spirits. Hoarding old ways and things is the opposite of freedom. That feeling of being suffocated is a sign that it's time to let go of things and open our hearts to something new. Sometimes that horrible feeling in our stomach is the divine push, telling us to let go. We have lugged it around for more than three moves, and it's time.

There is no better place to remember this lesson than in a community of women who come bearing nothing. A young woman once came to Thistle Farms with no earthly possessions other than her phone. A few weeks into her stay, she disappeared. The phone had pulled her back to the streets, because she had all her old johns and drug dealers in her contacts. Just that one possession from her past was too much. To get where she needed to be, she had to let go of even her phone.

An expression in the Gospel says, "The gate is narrow." I'd always thought it was kind of a judgmental expression, but in this case, a narrow gate was the path to freedom. The gate she needed to traverse was so narrow she couldn't even fit a phone through it.

* * *

"THREE MOVES ARE as good as a fire" is a gentle way of letting things go one step at a time. Watching it all go in real time is horrible. I once stood with a friend while her house was on fire and watched everything burn. She later talked about what it was like to let everything go. She said that as she stood there, all she kept thinking was that everyone she loved wasn't in that house. Everything else could be replaced. Then she laughed and called it an "immediate downsizing."

About ten years later, when she was forty-five, she died of breast cancer. She died on her couch after giving away everything that she had replaced after the fire, to all her friends as they came by to see her. Everything she collected after the fire, she offered to of us—shoes, dresses, crystals, and coats. In the end, it's all either trashed or given away. The old expression is that you never see a U-Haul behind a hearse. When she died way too soon, she taught her friends and family why it's good not to hold on to anything too tightly, except love.

* * *

THREE MOVES ALSO can be applied to letting go of things we're trying to accumulate, even before we have to store it! Saying the phrase before you make the purchase might stop you from buying it. You can ask yourself, *Do I want this? Will it just fill up my tiny 1920s closets in my house, and then I'll need to get it rid of it?* It almost always works.

A phrase my friend's mom, who is from the Bahamas, used to say to her sums up the idea of not needing to buy things. "Oh yeah, well, people in hell want iced tea." My friend said it was one of the nicer phrases her mom used to say when she wanted something. Say that before you hit the add to cart button and see if it doesn't save you some money.

We're always going to want things, but we don't necessarily need things, and things we once wanted so badly can be the very things that become a burden. My nephew says, "Boat owners are only happy two days: the day they buy the boat, and the day they sell it." Lugging and maintaining it brings little joy. My colleague at work, when anyone states that they'd like something, says simply, "that and a thousand loaves of bread," meaning the only thing that will satisfy your insatiable hunger for stuff is that and then another thousand loaves of bread. He is somewhat of a hermit though and probably can live on bread alone.

There are many takes on this idea. All of them can help you be free. The easiest and most recent example is when I saw a cheap pizza cooker that spins the pizza under a blazing heat lamp and cooks it. I loved everything about it and imagined having a pizza bar with all my sons and their girlfriends and building the pizza and watching them spin one by one on this cute appliance. So, I got it, and we had a coronavirus pizza birthday party. Then it sat on the counter for a few months and then I put it under the counter and eventually, I asked a friend if they wanted it, so they could have a socially distanced pizza bar party. It was a relief to see it out the door. I could have gotten another whole pizza dinner with the money I would have saved if I hadn't bought the shiny new object. This kind of thing is exactly why, for more than twenty years, I give up Target for Lent every single year. I can stop the madness of the moves before it starts, if I keep it simple.

*   *   *

FINALLY, I THINK three moves can be applied to letting go of old beliefs and politics that aren't life giving and freeing. I haven't looked up the word *stodgy*, but I am sure it means clinging to old junk so tightly that we no longer can move, and that makes us super grumpy. When I apply three moves to my worn-out truths, it translates into "believe less."

Our job on earth is to learn to love the world. We will lean into our truth when we can let go of thinking we have to convince the world to believe as we do or thinking we can never change what we believe. If the story we've created doesn't work for us anymore, if the god you have proclaimed has grown too small for all the wisdom you have gleaned from the crumbs you have collected, you can change. We can believe less of the dogma and institutional claims and live more faithfully with the remnant of our belief.

When we have come through pandemics, tornadoes, death, and a bombing in our personal and collective lives, it may well be that we emerge believing that less is more truthful, powerful, and beautiful.

Shortly before the 2020 presidential election, I was driving through the mountains in Montana with friends and having yet another conversation about the state of the world. My mind started drifting, as I'd had my fill of intellectual conversations on the theories of racism and disease in our country. I could feel that this wasn't a time for me to argue my old beliefs and hold them tightly, but in this time of shifting power, maybe the goal should be for me to listen and let go of anger that may give me heart disease or some other life-threating consequence.

We were out in Big Sky Country, with pines and forsaken old barns, and I started daydreaming about the Wild West and stories written about women who carried the beliefs of the world into this land. While the women during that era endured abuse, they kept the lies they'd been told, such as you have to please a powerful man, or your value is in how you can commodify your body, or if you want to keep your family, keep quiet. The shift in power evolved as women have been willing to let go of those garbage beliefs and exercising their God-given power and freedom.

About that time, we pulled up to a ghost town that we were going to hike through. The story of the town was that gold was found in the late 1800s, and at its peak, about one thousand people lived in the town, mining the hills for gold. To the north of the town had been a community of Irish immigrants, and a Chinese immigrant community was immediately to the south.

By the 1920s, the townspeople had mined more than two million dollars' worth of gold from the hills, mostly on the backs of the men and women they oppressed, and then they packed up and moved away. The Chinese immigrant community stayed on and continued to mine for the tiny bits of gold remaining. Then, a year later, the miners who had left came back and murdered the immigrants to take the last bits, and the whole place became a true ghost town, haunted by the secrets, violence, and beliefs of people claiming what was not theirs and believing they were entitled to it.

That is what happens when we believe we're right, no matter what, and we can take whatever we wish. There is death, and all that is left are ghosts. Believing less is the gift. Maybe if we believe in less dogma from institutions and more in the doggedness of love, we would be in paradise. We need to let go of the barriers that prevent us from loving the whole world. I know that I believe in fewer creedal expressions now than when I was ordained twenty-nine years ago, but what I am left believing I believe with my whole heart and will die trying to live into those beliefs.

We can let go. We can celebrate the truth that you never see a U-Haul behind a hearse. Whether it is an old story that haunts us, whether it is fear that we will be known, whether it is the deep grief we have been holding at bay, we can say, "free at last," even as we proclaim three moves are really as good as a fire.

●　　●　　●

THERE WAS A couple, like the thousands and thousands of couples around the world, that was struggling with how to get married during the coronavirus pandemic. Should we just have ten people? Should we wait? Should we livestream a service? The couple came to the chapel on a Sunday morning during the height of the pandemic, because he was the featured musician. We had just finished livestreaming the service, in which he sang an amazing blues song he'd written, while she was accompanying him on the piano with such wild abandon that all of us who were participating in the service were applauding and full of joy. The cameras turned off, and I commented about how it was so beautiful, and they said it was because they were in love and trying to figure out how to plan a wedding.

"Let's just do it now," I said kinda playfully. They looked at each other and said, yes, let's just take this moment, where the air is so thick with love's spirit that we can hardly cut through it, and get married. The other musicians who were there played some wedding music as we stood at the altar together. Five minutes later, with everyone in tears, they had gotten married.

The words they used to describe what happened were "giddy," and "floating," and "dizzy with love." They both were in their sixties, and both had been in recovery for more than twenty years. They knew themselves, and they knew the brokenness and aloneness of addiction and recovery. But that day, with no care about a dress or the flowers or the people or the liturgy, they had one of the most beautiful weddings I have witnessed. They stood there and looked at each other and wept tears of joy, while they took old rings and made them new by saying, "With all that I am and all that I have, I honor you." It wasn't even remotely about perfection—it was about recognizing and leaning into deep love.

They had let so much go that they had made way more than three moves. Probably more like three moves times seven. They had walked through the rubble of their lives and built new dreams. Three moves lets us have the chance to feel dizzy with love and to take bits and pieces of the rubble and make something practically divine.

RANT #3: LAUNDRY

I walked into the bathroom this morning when, for the umpteenth time, a pair of boxers belonging to one of my three sons was stuffed under the bottom shelf, where we stack the towels. All my sons, for all of their lives, stuff their boxers under that shelf after they shower and put a towel on. I think there is something wrong with them. They don't seem capable of carrying them to the laundry. "Am I paid to provide laundry service?" I ranted to my husband while gathering up the laundry and marching through the bedroom to the laundry room. "Why do they have to be reminded every damn time?" I said, loading a wash. "No one reminds me, and I know when laundry needs to be done. I have done all I can, and they are just awful young men."

As our youngest son started ascending the stairs, my husband yelled, "Hey, pick up your boxers—it's gross."

"God, honey, I didn't want you to say anything," I said. "He is struggling, because he is home from college because of COVID-19, and now he is going to be more depressed."

Rant #3: Laundry

My husband rolled his eyes internally and then said, "Okay."

I just needed to rant, I told him, then shut the washer and headed outside to open fields, where I could rant freely to trees.

EIGHT

The Feast

PAST THE LETTING GO lies the great feast, the feast where joy is poured out like fine wine, finally un-corked and rich. The feast happens at an open table, where business leaders proclaim how love thrives, and pastors preach with freedom about economic health. This feast isn't relegated to religious metaphor—it is the vision place that leads us to believe justice is a way of life, and it can flow like a river. This feast isn't just something to eat in the by and by; it is a driving force for us to share the bounty we have, to use our consumerism and power to help one another. And this feast isn't pitting lavishness against eco-nomics. It is the blending of the two in the truth that when we dwell together as brothers and sisters, there is more than we could have dreamed of alone. In the feast, the practically divine ultimately is celebrated, because it is where justice and peace are integrated into our lives.

After my mom died, I had a surprise dream about a feast. The dream was filled with such powerful images that I got out of bed and painted it. I still have the painting somewhere, tucked away with that tree made with her braid, along with a couple more treasures I haven't quite let go of, but that I am sure will be discarded within a week of my death. Yet the painting that looks like it was done by a semi-talented eight-year-old reminds me of the meaning of "feast."

In this book, I've written extensively about how, during my mom's entire life, she struggled to have enough money to keep it together. She didn't know that her greatest gift, born in the shadow of the widow's mite, was the way she shared everything she ever had. The great inheritance she left was that she lived so generously that there was really nothing to give in the end. There was never a debate among the five kids about who would take what. Instead, when we divvied up her things, we were saying things like, "You have to take the encyclopedias; I took the bicenten-nial plates." She never thought about her generosity—that was just how she was made. She was born with brown eyes, and she trusted there would be enough. Both were part of her genetic makeup. It was never as though she made a conscious decision to believe there would be enough. It was a given that with whatever we had, we could make a feast. We took old clothes and spent hours stripping them into long, braided strands to create amazing rugs as beautiful as Joseph's coat of many colors. We made luscious gardens from seeds and took whatever was left in the refrigerator, served it up on her old china, with fancy folded napkins, and made it feel like a party. When we dumped the canned olives into her old, fancy bowls, it was like a magic spell.

I loved her way of feasting with generosity, so when my husband, Marcus, got a check from the first country song he wrote that climbed the charts to number one, we made a plan. The song had been cut by Wynonna Judd and was called "Only Love." It was a song about how love is the only thing that will set us on the right course to lead us home, and the only thing we need to serve up a feast. We dreamed about what to do with the feast of money coming in. Immediately, I asked him to write my mom a card and put five one-hundred-dollar bills inside. He was all for it, but asked, "Don't you think she might think that it's kind of weird to get cash from me?"

"No," I said, smiling to beat the band. "She is going to love it."

When you have been cash poor your whole life, cash is a great gift! Cash can be a feast. Also included in the card were tickets to Jamaica, so all of us could take our first family vacation. Yup, we squandered almost the whole first check and made sure my mom was part of the squandering. We squandered it on the dream of a feast. We still have photos from that journey hanging on the wall, and our oldest son, who was four at the time, still remembers the papaya drinks with the umbrellas as his favorite of all time.

•   •   •

MY MOM WAS simple in dress and, as I've mentioned, wore her hair in a single braid down her back. Throughout her life, she struggled privately with her considerable weight. And she never spent money on herself, ever. Some evenings when I was growing up, I'd walk downstairs and there would be bills and the checkbook out, and she was hunched down with her strong hands holding up both sides of her head, like it was all too heavy. There were some painful times when she would get frustrated and lash out hitting. But she did it—she raised five kids as a single mom, working at a day care center, and made it as festive as possible. I am cognizant that, for the purpose of this story, I'm glossing over the violent outbursts she displayed during her most stressful times and the somewhat feral lifestyle we were raised in, but, dear God, she did it.

About four days after she died, I had a dream. It was like a hallucination you read about, animated with bright colors and soundtracks. The dream is full of details I won't ask you to read through, but the last scene in the dream is me standing on the end of a long, gray, wooden dock, while an African tribal leader and my mother stand in the back of a gondola, as they're being punted toward me by a young man in the front of the boat. My mother's hair is coiled in a lavish braid piled high on her head, like a crown. A red velvet cape with a cope of pure white fur is draped over her shoulder and extends to the ground. By her side, the young tribal leader is crowned, and it looks like they are a couple very much in love.

As the gondola drifts toward me, I notice a huge cornucopian feast filling the center of their boat, and I begin to cry. It's more than I can imagine. My mom doesn't get out of the boat and come over and hug me and tell me to stop. She only says, as the gondola pauses for a moment: "I'm happier than I have ever been. This is more than we ever imagined. I need to go." And she is then carried away. It's better than a chariot; it's better than a whirlwind. It's a gondola with a feast and a king. Good for her. In the dream, I was a side character, not even on her mind. She was free of even her five kids.

That dream is why I want the last saying that we carry with us from this writing to be, "This whole thing is a feast! It is practically divine."

*   *   *

THERE IS ENOUGH *to share.* Of all the old lessons and teachings, I am most grateful for this one. It's what keeps me from having to hold on to toilet paper during a pandemic or worry for the nonprofits in the summer. Proclaiming "There is enough" allows us to go out and build something new. It means we can dream of building a shelter like a cathedral and not be laughed out of the room. I know that, in the end, it is about love, and there is enough love to carry us all through. There is more than enough mercy and forgiveness to go around and to offer to one another in love.

There have been a thousand other people besides my mom who have practiced the miracle of feasts, where others might preach famine. For instance, I think of the women in Greece in the refugee camp, who, on our fifth night, laid out a spread fit for kings. We were finishing our day of weaving, when some wooden tables made from old pallets were placed between the endless rows of containers the refugees were housed in. Chairs were pieced together from discarded two-by-fours, and thick plastic came out of various dwellings.

Everyone was filled with joy. For a minute, we stopped all the worry and seemingly endless trauma, and we laughed and stuffed our faces. For a brief moment, between courses, there was no war, no poverty, no grieving. All those things would all flood back in as soon as the plates were cleared, but during that feast, we could celebrate that, for a minute, love was overflowing.

Around that table, I sampled all the food, made huge gestures about how much I loved everything, and felt on the verge of tears and laughter the whole time. I think I knew, sitting there, that this was kind of like a marriage feast, that eating together like this was bonding us for the long haul, and what we were committing to was going to be years of hard work. I loved it though. I loved it so much.

I wouldn't have missed that feast for the world. Just writing about it makes me hunger for another.

Don't you long for the feast? For the big table where we just slide in more chairs as people come up? Don't lose that vision, come hell or high water. Come fires, tornadoes, a bomb on Christmas morning, pandemics, or protests. Don't let the wonder of the vision of the cornucopia pouring out justice fade against the gray morning of another workday. It has been and remains critical in our common work for justice and peace. We cannot skip over the feast part, even when it's slim pickings. It is too important in the work of living practically divine. The feast is where we are fed and where we stop and refresh. The feast is woven into business, school, religious traditions, and family life.

There are countless visions of feasts, and dreaming about them fills your cup with joy. If you ever start muttering phrases like "another day, another dollar" about the rut and monotony of daily tasks, take five, and dream of a feast. It will pull you up from the ditch and set you on higher ground.

Recently, I dreamed of a feast set on the Chobe River in Botswana. I dreamed of it so specifically that I contacted the property manager there and started a secret plan to return to that riverside. I think the dream of the feast rose in the long pandemic, which breathed new life into so many of the divisions in the world that feel immutable. Centuries of colonialism and slavery make it seem impossible that there's a table where all are welcome, and reconciliation is poured out like gravy over biscuits.

My dreamy feast would start in the first place I was an intern for my pastoring career, Gaborone, Botswana. That was the place I got lost in my ministry, where I learned about AIDS, and where I experienced the sun and moon and Venus in a perfect triangle at sunrise. It was the place where I discovered that the desert holds life, and that there is a feast of a thousand shades of brown in the Kalahari. It is the place I began to understand the relationship between economic development and politics, as my father-in-law was the director of the United States aid program there for years. Marcus's parents used to take us to the Chobe on vacation, after we'd all left the city of Gaborone and our work with the church and hospice. On our first visit to the Chobe River, Marcus's father told me that Elizabeth Taylor had honeymooned at the nearby hotel. It made the whole experience feel romantic and extravagant.

The feast vision begins with a long table on a lawn by the Chobe River in northern Botswana, near a small church that serves visitors and residents. To get to the feast, you have to walk down a short, cobbled path, lined with budding trees with new, thin, pale green leaves filled with sunlight. This path ensures that our intentions at the feast are for radical forgiveness, with love pouring out. It also gives us time to unburden ourselves from all the things we can't bring to that feast.

The long table is made by pushing several tables from various homes together and then covering them all in a long, brightly colored, designed cloth from neighboring Tanzania. The cloth reminds us of the sacred nature of what we are about to partake in. It is unifying and stunning. Designed, stamped, and crafted by women's hands, it brings to this table hope for women's justice. It is set out like a buffet, with baskets of offerings the growing crowd can't possibly consume completely. It is more than any of us thought would be there. It is the miracle of potluck, the wonder of stone soup foretold in stories.

Standing before the great bounty isn't about stuffing as much into our bodies as we can, but savoring new tastes that widen our palates. Some of the dishes are made to quench our racing minds. Some breads are there to dip into the deep well of longing we carry within us and sate our sadness. There are even dishes to inspire us to act and work, even though we fear the critique of others.

The real feast begins with a parade of people coming from every corner of the world, and other people stand along the path and cheer. In that parade are amazing women leaders and advocates and survivors. Soon the parade stops, and we all fill our plates and sit in the shade of the enormous old baobab trunk that has been resting here for a thousand years. It is big enough to shade us all, and everyone feels welcome. The people at the feast are from every creed and no creed. They represent the entire Crayola possibility of skin tones. There are older women like me, and young women who are dreaming new dreams under that symbol of bounty and positivity.

Someone begins a song that seems to call all of us to stay and restore our souls while we fill our bellies. The lyrics are caught up in a sweeping melody and speak of sweet peace lying on the other side of our work. At the end of the song, a huge sun is setting in bands of blended orange and pink that have melded into the color of heaven. There are no more shadows, just the sun bowing to kiss us good evening.

Elephants are downriver, playing at the edge with one of their babies. As we begin to say goodbye, with clouds backlit by the memory of the sun, we start to offer toasts to all that we love. The feast ends with tears of deep gratitude mixed into the bottom of the wine glass. We know we can't stay at the feast, yet this acknowledgment doesn't make the experience sad—it makes it rich. Everyone there knows we are all merely passing through, to fill our cups and then head back out.

The miracle is that you can imagine a feast on your next breath. In that vision, neither separation nor death prevents someone from coming to dine with you. Let yourself imagine it all, and delight in the details and colors. I believe that a feast without a fast is gluttony, but a fast without a feast makes us just as sick. When we keep the vision of the feast before us, we can weather the leaner pickings of the day.

• • •

AS WE FACE the continued challenges from the way that stress has been stoked by the flames of turmoil, we should call up a peace feast, with deep, pulsing rhythms that allow us to sway and breathe. We have been told there is a peace that passes understanding. A feast of peace dwells in the sweet and sacred space we can find even in the midst of hard times. A peace that passes understanding means we cannot attain it through a rigorous thought process.

This kind of peace can come in the midst of war and injustice. We've all read stories of heroic men and women who, amid chaos and oppression, speak of a peace that keeps their hearts and minds in the knowledge of love. This is a kind of peace that surrenders to the reality of our circumstances instead of fighting it. In the world of recovery, it is called *radical acceptance*. This is a kind of peace that digs below the surface of anger, fear, and hate, to cultivate the fertile soil that can birth hope and acceptance and love. It lives in the truth that we must all root to rise. This is a kind of peace that claims the power of peace that dwells in us, even as we strive to believe that it's possible. It is easier to say, "I have no peace," than to claim, "I have deep peace in me." This is the kind of peace that searches for reconciliation and forgiveness in community. A peace that lives into the deepest memory of how we were once all family. This is the kind of peace that desires to share peace like a feast, with brothers and sisters who share our desire to live in love. We have been working toward peace for years, so it is not far from us.

*   *   *

WE CAN FEAST on peace this day, if we desire to conjure it up. I remember when the pandemic landed in our house in the summer of 2020, from one of our son's friends, and I got sick. At first, I thought I had sun poisoning, but as the aching and fever worsened during the day, it dawned on me that I probably had COVID-19. The hardest part wasn't feeling sick but worrying that I might get a lot sicker. I kept thinking, *You're younger—you'll be fine.* But then I'd think of my twelve-year-old self up in a willow tree sneaking a cigarette, and I'd think, *I wonder how bad this is going to get.* My chest felt tight for a couple days, and I believe my sense of smell and taste are partially gone for the long haul.

Three out of five of us in my household got sick days apart, and all I could think about was making sure we all stayed home and got better. But I also dreamed of when we'd all feel better and how I wanted to celebrate with crab legs and fresh veggies from our garden. I'd dream of feeling peaceful and calm in the midst of the worrying that wanted to be my only companion.

The fatigue and aches passed in a couple days, but on day three of "The Covid," one of the great graduates of the residential program at Thistle Farms called me from the emergency room. She was being admitted for coronavirus and felt herself panicking. She told me she couldn't breathe. If 2020 had a battle cry, that was it: "I can't breathe." While I could breathe, I could easily empathize with her as I felt my lungs tight against my chest when I inhaled, like there was a weight sitting on me.

She and I sat on the phone and conspired (breathed together) to create a feast of peace. Our feast began with the declaration that there was no crying at a peace feast. Then in slow and rhythmic words, we reminded one another of all the scriptures we knew about peace. We recited them back and forth, leaving space for breathing. Her feast was unfolding while she was in a hospital bed, so we imagined all the people praying that she could relax into that bed. She was feasting on peace as she began to feel herself relaxing into their bed of prayers. That bed was strong enough to hold her up. She could feel it pressing up on her, and her whole body relaxing into the form of the bed. Then we stopped talking and kept breathing with concentration.

I whispered to her that I wouldn't hang up until the doctor came in. A few seconds later, she said her child was calling and she needed to go, and she assured me she was going to get through this by remembering to be at peace. I felt so much better myself after feasting on peace, and I hadn't left my house. It is a wondrous gift that we can soothe one another, even through our own state of being broken and bruised.

* * *

A FEAST DOESN'T have to be elaborate. It might be as simple as bag of potato chips. One day in Nashville, a woman was walking by one of the residential homes that's part of Thistle Farms, while three of us were sitting on the porch. She looked hungry and defeated. All we had was a bag of chips, and one of the women got up and gave it to her. For the next month, whenever she walked by, someone at the house would give her chips or a bottle of water or maybe a granola bar. Each visit, the conversation deepened as trust started building, and she moved closer to the porch. She moved into the house the next month, and her life changed forever.

She graduated two years later, with a car and house and a good job. She still keeps chips in her car to offer women she passes, because she knows that a bag of chips was the beginning of her feast. That bag of chips was the beginning of new relationships, a new job, a new home, new friends, and a new way of living.

Part of the struggle for folks wanting to get involved is thinking the issues are too big, and I am too small. All I have is a bag of chips, and hungry people are on street corners all over. The overwhelming feeling is inadequacy, so we keep the chips in the pantry and turn away when we see someone looking hungry. Worse yet, we wonder who on God's green earth even cares if I give my chips away or store them for the next storm. It makes no difference in the balance of hunger in the world if I keep my chips or

give them away. That is just ridiculous. Of course it makes
a difference.

There's a quote attributed to Mother Teresa about doing small acts with great love. She picked up that idea
from Saint Catherine of Siena, who said our calling was to
do small things with great love, and even small acts of love
change the scales of love in the world. And she got that
idea from the motherline of wisdom, which has passed
down that truth since time began. That motherline con-
veys that even a small offering of food keeps the world
sated. We don't need to be afraid or look the other way or
cross the street when we see the hungry person in front of
us. All we're required to do for the feast is some small
thing with great love. Do what you can. Give a bag of chips.

· · ·

THE STORY OF handing a woman a bag of chips and
discovering it's the beginning of a feast isn't a unique
story. How many feasts have you been able to find because
someone gave you a small kindness? None of us were born
knowing how to feed ourselves. Someone gave us the
equivalent of a bag of chips, which sustained us and gave
us life. In turn, we instinctively know how important
those offerings are. We know, like we know to cover our
heads when someone yells, "Duck," that giving people the
time and space and resources they need to take the next
step is at the heart of love. The realm of feasting doesn't
call for heroes—it calls for gracious hosts to prepare the

meal, set the table, and clean up. Hospitality is a virtue that embodies the essence of love. In hospitality, I think intention is the lion's share of feast making. If our intention is loving and welcoming, we offer a feast; if it's resentful and angry, no matter what we serve, it will be bitter.

The other morning, I was cleaning my kitchen and wiping down all the surfaces and thinking about why I was doing it. I was doing it as an act of love for my sister who was coming by, so she'd feel welcome at the table; for my husband, who may not notice but will still be grateful for the sense of order; and for my son's girlfriend, who was stopping by to pick something up. It made the cleaning more like a small act of worship. Holding those folks in my heart while I unloaded the dishwasher and got down on my knees to scrub the tile didn't make me resentful—it made me grateful. I wish I could clean like that all the time. Preparation is nine-tenths of the feast, and to move through that with love changes the whole feast. At times I've prepared with less noble feelings, and I wonder if this resulted in any bitter aftertaste in the food.

Early in my marriage, I recall visiting my husband's family. After an amazing meal, his mom would get up from the table and start doing the dishes. Then she'd comment ever so slightly about how she wished for more help. Such a comment from a kind, loving, and gracious host turned my stomach enough to be on edge for the evening. We laughed about it for years afterward, and I'd make a habit of jumping up after we ate, and she'd say, "Relax—it's okay." I still think it would have been better to sit around the table with dirty dishes and laugh for a while and clean up later.

Implicit in the message of "feast" is to serve in love. Find that sweet spot where the world's needs meet your great desires, as theologian Frederick Buechner put it. For me, I found the place where I can be a pretty good host at the intersection of crafts and justice. There is a place for you where the intersection between your vocation, talents, passions, and skills meet in sweet communion—you should set a table in that place. If it means saying a prayer, find the first word. If it means running a race, train. What it means is that you can make a small change that makes a big difference. You can stand on new ground and believe you are not lost. The distance between the desert and the garden is much smaller than we think. When we get to the garden, we get to feast, bask, and enjoy it! We can't do everything, and we can't do things perfectly. But we can find our divine purpose in practical ways.

*   *   *

EVERYONE WHO ACCEPTS chips, prepares the meal, cleans up, and comes hungry becomes the hero of their own story at a feast. Shelia Simpkins came to Thistle Farms as a young woman from an outreach on the streets of Nashville. A group of volunteers would take tables and cloths, cookies and casseroles, and set a table on one of the notable streets where the women walked. We set up chairs and offered goodie bags and manicures as well, for anyone who wanted one. It was a mobile feast that helped women out there know there was another option.

Shelia was offered a square of casserole, and she sat down and started talking to one of the volunteers. She said she couldn't believe the connection she felt, and she wanted to come home to Thistle Farms right then. It took her another couple of months to make her way into one of the houses, but she said that the conversation and casserole had stuck with her. She was ready to make a change.

Three months after she moved in, she was diagnosed with breast cancer. She was just thirty-five years old and needed a lumpectomy, chemotherapy, and radiation. Shelia had the most beautiful head of hair, and during her treatment, she lost every bit of it. When we talked for the first time after she was bald, I mentioned to her that the scars on her head looked like a road map.

She said: "It does. It's a map of all the violence I have taken from the abusive men in my life since I was six." Her mother first started conditioning her, at six years old, to satisfy men. While Shelia was performing oral sex on the man, Shelia's mother would tell her to suck on it like it was a lollipop. When Shelia got her head bashed in, her trafficker wouldn't take her to the doctor; he just stuck her head under cold water until the bleeding stopped.

Shelia survived the cancer, got well, was married in my living room, had two beautiful children, and earned both undergraduate and graduate degrees. But she was just getting started. She became the head of the national network for Thistle Farms and has helped open another three hundred beds for women survivors around the country, and that number grows every year. She took the crumbs of her life and is cooking up an incredible feast with the simple ingredients of love, hard work, and hospitality. She is serving up a feast none of us imagined, and it's such a gift to still get invited to sit at her table. This world doesn't need more heroes—it needs good hosts.

I'm not sure when it happens that the person you thought you were serving becomes the person inviting you to dine, but that is a feast I never want to miss.

Recently, I was painting one of the residential houses with my sons and husband, when Shelia walked in with water for us. The air-conditioning in the house was out, and the thermometer read ninety-nine degrees. She came and gave us the very thing we needed for a feast, and she greeted and loved on my family and told us she was proud of us. I can't imagine anything finer, and I thanked her for sticking through the decades of work and still offering so much love to us.

It is what love truly looks like. The line between the giver and the receiver is erased, and this is practically divine. At the feast, all the lines are blurred. The line between priest and prostitute, between beggar and patron, between us and them. There is no founder of the feast who always and forever has to preside. We serve one another at different feasts. The feast isn't an authoritarian model, which is why prisons and politics get so sick. The feast is a shared hosting, where we serve one another so we all can eat.

* * *

WE DESERVE TO sit at the table and feast on love. We have done what we have done, and we have had done to us what has been done to us. We have had enough shame where we just eat from the crumbs that fall. It's time to sit and eat at the table with everybody else who is holy imperfect.

In every space we find ourselves, no matter how mundane, how painful, or even how sweet, the feast comes when we accept the most divine truth: we are loved. That is the practically divine experience, when we can be who we are and where we are seen for who we are.

I have a dear friend who signs her emails to me as "your sister." The world knows this sister as a man, husband, and grandfather. For decades we have forged a friendship in which she feels safe enough to be herself and dine with me on a feast of sisterhood. We love so many of the same things and can share stories and images for days.

Once, she shared a story with me about growing up in Arkansas and finding her grandmother's old silk slip in a trunk. She doesn't know why, but she took it and decided that if anyone asked her about it, she'd say it was for Halloween. The private and sacred feast for my beloved sister was one piece of old, discarded clothing she could hold and help her find her way to feast with safe people to be herself. She has taught me volumes about the need for people to find a table where they are welcomed and loved.

She has also taught me that there is no feast where justice isn't present. It's just a big meal. Justice isn't a sideline offered; it is central to a love feast. At our feast, my hope is for us to learn to make justice our way of life. This past year, I served an online tea party feast to 1,500 people who'd signed up to drink a cup of healing tea together. It was a feast of an enormous size, and what everyone was the hungriest for was justice! They were starving for a grounded justice that is deep and powerful enough to call out from arid mountains for all of us to work for a river flowing way off in the valley. They wanted a justice steeped in subversive joy. They were asking for a justice that can filter into their whole lives. We all need justice at the feast that impacts what we consume, what we pour out, and how we devote our energy. Justice isn't what we do after we do everything else. It is a way of life.

I still have miles to go to live a more just life, but I hope we can all stop and smell the rose justice tea while we're inching our way to the promised land. Tea and justice are consummate hosts, serving hospitality on lavish tables. Justice and tea go together like bread and wine.

*   *   *

ON THIS JOURNEY you have taken with me through this book of experiencing the practically divine in our ordinary lives in extraordinary ways, let me leave you with one final thought: Take a breath before you close this chapter. Breathe in the air life has given you. Breathe out a word of gratitude for some small act you were able to do in love. Then breathe in again, and remember some small act you were able to receive in love.

Think of a morning where the clouds hung in the air like there was nowhere for them to go, and they lingered. On your next couple breaths, take in the kind of lingering, thick air, and as you breathe out, release whatever word was formed in that thick space that can ferment a thought. Breathe those words out. Continue to breathe in and out until, perhaps by grace, you feast on a new thought, original and divine, that rose from your spirit.

When we move past the thoughts that come quickly and focus on those that linger in rhythm with our breath and life, we are practically divine. When we breathe in practically and breathe out divine, we are in tune with the cicadas hanging out in the trees. We are clear like unriled creek water, where the dirt has settled to the bottom. We are like the earth spinning wildly and in perfect sync with the universe's trajectory.

If that sounds like I've overstated it, I don't think I have. If anything, I think I have downplayed the enormous possibilities of a world in which we recognize ourselves and one another as practically divine. In that world, there would be enough food to feed all the children. In this world, there is enough food, but the injustice is in the distribution of that food. In that world, there would be no physical and sexual trauma for children. In this world, it fills our prisons with its survivors. In that world, politicians from all persuasions would hear the cries of the poor, and war would cease, because no one could bear the cries. In this world, we send our youth to war, because they will do our killing for us.

That world is closer than we may imagine. The wilderness is closer to Jerusalem than we think. It is a matter of making justice our way of life and living practically divine for the sake of the whole world in our own small way, with nothing but gratitude rising from our imperfectly perfect lips. Amen.

PRACTICALLY DIVINE

We are made of stardust, oceans, and dirt.

Knit together in the secret place,

Woven from the depths of the earth,

We are a little less than angels, practically divine.

We are born poetic, like drops of dew

Catching sunlight and throwing rainbows.

We grow up, curious as wild cubs

Howling at night,

Hearing distant laments that echo our longing.

We are raised to scan clouds for signs

Then told to plant our feet in soil.

In youth we are as expectant as acorns,

Holding hundred-year-oaks in our belly.

In parenting we are as practical as hyenas,

Serving up feasts from leftovers.

In old age we transform from nymph to dragonfly

Flapping translucent wings, hovering on puffs of hope.

We are made in love, then take on flesh and bone

That grounds us like a broken wing on a hawk.

Our voices raise in praise and petition

For our transient green valley.

We hew a life from sweat blended with old earth.

We are practically divine,

Almost and just enough.

Acknowledgments

THANK YOU WITH MY whole heart to the women of Thistle Farms, who have been my patient teachers in all things practical and divine.

I never would have written this book without my assistant, Kristin Beckum, who is growing a movement for women's freedom while she raises three beautiful girls!

I'm in love with my agent, Amy Hughes, and all the amazing people at Harper Horizon, especially Publisher Andrea Fleck-Nisbet and Amanda Bauch, the best editor I have ever worked with.

My gratitude to the people at Thistle Farms and all our partner communities who kept working for justice amid the pandemic.

Many thanks to the community of St. Augustine's Chapel, especially my co-priest Scott Owings.

To Hal Cato and all the leaders at Thistle Farms Global, I am grateful that we laugh as much as we cry in serving survivors.

I am deeply grateful to all the boards I work with, who help keep me humble, especially the global board lead by Frannie Kieschnick, Lori Barra, Fiona Prine, and Laurie Platek. Dreaming with you is the greatest gift I have known.

I'm grateful to all the PR folks who are social media advocates spreading the news that love is the most powerful force for change, including Val Holden and Marlei Olson.

Thank you to Mike Kinman, Chip Edens, Lila Galloway, Andy Doyle, Michael Curry, Nicholas Hitimana, Phoebe Roff, Glenda Curry, Hill Carmichael, and all the other leaders of faith who are brave enough to lead with love.

I'm super grateful to Tara Armistead and everyone who has taught me to see the holiness in a flower.

Acknowledgments

My appreciation to my family, especially Levi, Caney, Moses, Dallas, and Katherine, who made quarantine a party. Thank you for teaching me to play "ring of fire" and forgiving me for making mint juleps with cilantro.

I love you, Marcus Hummon, and believe you, above all others, have reminded me that the closest I can get to fathoming the eternal in this life is in the moments of bliss we have shared for decades. You are the gift.

About the Author

BECCA STEVENS is an Episcopal priest, survivor of childhood sexual abuse, social justice innovator, and tireless advocate for women survivors in her hometown of Nashville, Tennessee, and around the world. Her belief that love heals is the underlying theme behind everything she does. *Practically Divine* serves not only to deliver this message to more people but to show how—in real life, in all its darkness and lightness, and in real people, in all their brokenness and giftedness—we can find, experience, and share love. She describes her life as an average-sized glass overflowing with love.

Becca is her mother's daughter, practical and crafty. She is her father's daughter, searching for meaning with an old compass. She has been married for thirty-two years to Marcus Hummon, a Grammy-winning and Hall of Fame songwriter. Together they have raised three sons, all artists in their own rights. Their home is filled with music, paintings, designs, and too many dogs.

Becca has founded ten justice organizations around the world and has helped raise more than $58 million to lift women out of poverty and into freedom. She is a dynamic speaker and spirited leader who is in high demand for appearances at events across the globe. She offers keynote speeches, leads workshops, appears in countless media outlets, is the president of Thistle Farms, heads the national network of its sister organizations, and helps support her home chapel in Nashville, Tennessee.

Becca has been featured everywhere, from NPR to the *New York Times*, *Today*, and *ABC World News*. She has been recognized as a Top 10 CNN Hero and a White House Champion of Change. She has experienced and listened to stories from women all over the world, always finding more signs of God's love in even the most horrific circumstances. Those stories often bring as much laughter as tears. Her work is her joy.

About Thistle Farms

Becca founded Thistle Farms twenty-five years ago as a community for survivors of trafficking, prostitution, and addiction. At its Nashville headquarters, Thistle Farms continues to provide a haven for survivors with six homes, a café, a retail store, and an emergency safe house. Thistle Farms has become a global movement for women's freedom, with a growing network including five hundred free, long-term beds for survivors, as well as a marketplace with more than 1,800 artisan survivors contributing globally. Thistle Farms Global Market is a one-stop shop, with partners from Nepal to Kenya to Rwanda to Greece to Mexico to India. The latest collaboration is with a women's group in Belize, building the first long-term house there for women.

Thistle Farms is a multifaceted justice enterprise that employs survivor leaders who have dedicated their lives to helping more women. The organization is a thriving example of what embracing the practically divine in our lives can blossom into. It started as an idea to share the most basic, practical needs, and it now changes lives around the world.